Zilch

NANCY LUBLIN

THE POWER OF
ZERO IN BUSINESS

PORTFOLIO

PORTFOLIO
Published by the Penguin Group
Penguin Group (USA) Inc., 375 Hudson Street,
New York, New York 10014, U.S.A.
Penguin Group (Canada), 90 Eglinton Avenue East, Suite 700,
Toronto, Ontario, Canada M4P 2Y3
(a division of Pearson Penguin Canada Inc.)
Penguin Books Ltd, 80 Strand, London WC2R 0RL, England
Penguin Ireland, 25 St. Stephen's Green, Dublin 2, Ireland
(a division of Penguin Books Ltd)
Penguin Books Australia Ltd, 250 Camberwell Road, Camberwell,
Victoria 3124, Australia
(a division of Pearson Australia Group Pty Ltd)
Penguin Books India Pvt Ltd, 11 Community Centre, Panchsheel Park,
New Delhi – 110 017, India
Penguin Group (NZ), 67 Apollo Drive, Rosedale, North Shore 0632,
New Zealand (a division of Pearson New Zealand Ltd)
Penguin Books (South Africa) (Pty) Ltd, 24 Sturdee Avenue,
Rosebank, Johannesburg 2196, South Africa

Penguin Books Ltd, Registered Offices:
80 Strand, London WC2R 0RL, England

First published in 2010 by Portfolio,
a member of Penguin Group (USA) Inc.

10 9 8 7 6 5 4 3 2

LIBRARY OF CONGRESS CATALOGING-IN-PUBLICATION DATA

Lublin, Nancy,———
 Zilch : the power of zero in business / Nancy Lublin.
 p. cm.
 Includes index.
 ISBN 978-1-59184-314-6
 1. Nonprofit organizations. 2. Organizational effectiveness. 3. Performance. 4. Work—Psychological
aspects. I. Title.
 HD62.6.L83 2010
 658—dc22 2009046452

Printed in the United States of America
Set in Elegant Garamond BT
Designed by Sabrina Bowers

FOR MY DAD

CONTENTS

Zilch

INTRODUCTION

RECENTLY I WAS IN a meeting at the offices of a ginormous global conglomerate. Eight of us sat around a big, beautiful table made of incredible wood no doubt harvested from some disappearing rain forest. A fancy phone in the middle of the table linked us to voices from three other cities—the media buyer for the company, a rep from the creative firm, and a brand strategist. They served the most amazing oversized oatmeal cookies with white chocolate chips that were still warm, the sweet scent filling the room. We were discussing the launch of a new campaign, so the mood should have been corks-popping celebratory. But just the day before, the corporation's media budget had been "slashed." Everyone in the room was either dejected or in panic. The disembodied voices on the phone were mumbling mournfully to each other.

The most practical thinkers in the room—I counted two—remained hopeful, searching for solutions to this annoying little problem of having "zilch." (Note: The advertising budget had been

slashed to a mere $2 million.) The top exec in the room—who was wearing a pair of handcrafted leather shoes so incredibly lovely that the left shoe alone could have been sold on eBay and fed a family of six in Rwanda for a year—announced that he had the answer: the team would call other departments and try to cobble the money together (another "paltry" $1.5 million) by cannibalizing from other budget lines. Everyone agreed. One team member immediately poked at her BlackBerry; "I'm on it," she grunted. "I know the sports marketing group can pull some T&E funds, and global marketing should be able to free up something too." Everyone looked relieved. The best response to not having enough money for advertising? Apparently, get more money.

Not having money is familiar turf for me, although this ostensible solution of theirs was not. I've spent my career running not-for-profit organizations that do not have a-gazillion-and-one budget lines from which to steal dollars. So I gently stuck my toe into the boiling water and ventured some suggestions that I thought might be both smart and cost-effective. "Have you thought about using free online tools like Twitter to promote this campaign?" Silence. "Have you thought about leveraging partnerships as distribution channels?" More silence. "Maybe we could create an event, or hook into a rising trend so that we can generate free buzz from news outlets?"

They looked at me, silently, as if I had three eyes and six arms and were the firstborn spawn of beings from another planet. *Who is this weird creature? What language is she speaking? How did she get past security?*

So I responded to their silence with some of my own. Sitting there, I had an epiphany: *I think differently. I'm not like them.* Maybe I am an alien. I'm from a weird place: the Land of Zilch. But I'm not alone. In fact, I don't think I'm particularly gifted. There are lots of freaks like me—we're called not-for-profit business leaders.

Simply put, really great not-for-profits are brilliant at doing more with less. We understand the power of zero.

We motivate employees to work past five o'clock with commit-

ment, creativity, and passion totally disproportionate to their tiny salaries.

We engage our board members to truly add value to our companies. We don't pay them a dime—and actually, most of them pay us!

We skillfully land donors (a.k.a. customers) with an artful ask and the promise of getting almost nothing in return other than the knowledge of—and warm fuzzies from—doing something good.

We manage volunteers and get them to produce amazing results—say, houses or playgrounds or millions of dollars in revenue—without a competitive interview process, financial compensation, or the threat of termination.

So instead of standing on my head or doing cartwheels down the center of the table in this plush corporate-headquarters meeting room—I didn't want to destroy all those beautiful cookies—I decided to write down all the lessons they could learn from me, the alien not-for-profit girl. I decided to write a book—and I decided that it would have to be a business book, because that is my experience: I have run not-for-profit businesses for the past seventeen years.

If you are expecting a book about doing more good, you've got the wrong book. This isn't going to be a lecture about how corporations should contribute more to society. This book is not going to mention the terms *Zen* or *mission*. It is not a spiritual tome about finding yourself or generating good karma—I want you to read with a highlighter in hand, not a candle.

Everyone loves to talk about how not-for-profits need to behave more like businesses. They're right. We've read the literature, and we've studied best practices—I used the Harvard Business School case study on Dunkin' Donuts to help me franchise Dress for Success, which I started in 1996. We've hired great people from the business world to come lead our organizations, bringing those best practices in-house. We've even learned to charge for our services, monetize our core competencies, and create sustainable enterprises. By retracing the footprints of the for-profit world, we've learned to

think of ourselves as more than just change agents—we're change companies. We're transformers.

We've all watched recently as giant for-profit companies, many of them with invaluable brands and incredible histories, have collapsed. Perhaps we should call them *nonprofits*? I've seen CEOs and COOs make executive errors and operational mistakes that no not-for-profit leader worth his salt would make.

Sure, not every for-profit company is readying a bankruptcy filing and ordering cardboard boxes in bulk. But even those companies that aren't imploding seem to be slimming budgets, hunting for new and more effective strategies, and striving to squeeze just a little more productivity out of that ever-smaller staff. Everyone is counting their pennies, making sure to extract value from every last cent.

These are things that we in the not-for-profit world have been doing for years, and after years and years of being told that we in the not-for-profit sector need to be more structured, more profitable, more strategic, and more like organizations in the corporate world, the pendulum is now swinging in the other direction. Now we not-for-profits have much to offer organizations that are willing to listen and learn.

I started talking to friends at other not-for-profits, asking them to identify the tricks of our trade that might be useful to share. I realized that what we have to offer can be boiled down to one concept: *the power of zero*. We get more done with less of just about everything from our people to our money to our workplaces to our vendors. Starting with zero isn't a problem for us. It's a challenge that we rise to every day. Zilch is what drives us to be more innovative, more passionate, more creative. Stop whining about your budget cuts and start asking yourself what you would do if you had zilch. You'll be surprised to discover just how powerful that is.

I'm not going to suggest that not-for-profits have all the answers or that our approach always translates to the corporate side. We're not perfect either! But there is value, for leaders of all stripes, in looking at best practices in the business of not-for-profit management.

Unlike big business, we not-for-profits may not be able to grow through acquisition, but we do know how to grow through alliance.

Unlike big business, we may not be able to promote people based on their experience and competencies, but we can identify employees with fire in their belly and put them in positions to blaze their own trails.

Unlike big business, we may not be proficient in creating brands through research and focus groups, but we're positively brilliant at creating brands by being unique, simple, consistent, and relevant.

Like smart businesses, we're going to survive and succeed by innovating and delivering results—and over the past decade, many not-for-profits have delivered outstanding, world-changing, awe-inspiring results. You may be surprised by how ubiquitous and how influential we've become, and I'm not talking about our storied behemoths like the Red Cross and the Salvation Army. No, I'm thinking of some of the greatest new companies of the last ten years—brands that have quickly become household names and created seemingly irreplaceable products. Several of them are not-for-profits, including Wikipedia and Mozilla (creator of the Web browser Firefox).

Let me get a necessary caveat out of the way: some not-for-profits are lousy. Of course they are. And some not-for-profit leaders are tired lame ducks. Obviously. We're not going to talk about them because I didn't interview those companies and those executives. Instead, I selected an international list of not-for-profit rock stars, including Charles Best from DonorsChoose, Wendy Kopp from Teach For America, Jimmy Wales from Wikipedia, Greg Baldwin from VolunteerMatch, John Lilly from Mozilla, Zainab Salbi from Women for Women International, and more than a dozen others. Their stories and strategies are sprinkled throughout this book, alongside my own thoughts, which draw on my experience founding Dress for Success and leading the largest organization in America for teens and social change, DoSomething.org. I am grateful to these people not only for their time and their candor but also for

their camaraderie. It's nice to know that, even if I'm an alien, at least I'm an alien with good, like-minded peers.

From our shared experience, I've drawn eleven major themes. Why eleven? It's a number that's significant to me because in the not-for-profit world, I like to say that we don't stop at ten. Ten is never enough. Everyone else shoots for "one to ten." In the not-for-profit world, we start with zero and deliver an eleven. If an unpaid intern comes to me and asks how hard he needs to work to make something happen, I don't say twice or three times or even ten times as hard. Want to succeed in this business? Then work to the power of eleven and pay for zero.

1

DO MORE WITH LESS CASH TO THROW AT PEOPLE

FOR YEARS, CONVENTIONAL CORPORATE wisdom has dictated that the more you pay your employees, the more value you will extract from them. We have only to look back to 2008 to see how supremely wrong that alleged wisdom is. It was an *annus horribilis* for Wall Street. Bear Stearns and Lehman Brothers ceased to exist; firms that did survive lost billions upon billions of dollars; and billions more in market cap—and shareholder savings—evaporated. Yet employees at Wall Street firms still took home an estimated total of $18.4 billion in bonuses, the sixth-largest haul on record. And according to the most recent Financial Executive Compensation Survey, the average base salary in that sector actually went up 3.7 percent. Whatever happened to performance-based pay?

Here's the simple truth: salary doesn't equal great performance or stellar productivity. Show me ten people who truly love what they're doing and who understand why they're doing it. I'd bet that they outwork, out-innovate, and outperform ten other people who

are paid twice as much but lack this love and understanding. Historically, money has been a bigger motivator, but other factors are acquiring equal or even greater status. Frances Hesselbein, the former CEO of the Girl Scouts who also chaired the board of the Peter F. Drucker Foundation for Nonprofit Management, says, "Few people are motivated only by money. The most motivated workers are those whose personal goals are congruent with the company's goals." Most individuals want more out of life than money—they want everything from spiritual fulfillment to a sense of personal accomplishment to the prestige of affiliation with success. Our society has changed, and yet corporations have not changed along with it.

Did you know that, in a recent AMP/Cone study, 77 percent of respondents said that a company's social commitment is an important factor in selecting a job? Furthermore, according to Cone, Americans expect companies to adopt a socially responsible attitude regardless of economic climate; in other words, the bottom line isn't the only or primary bottom line, and money isn't always what matters most. People want to do something meaningful with their lives, and they want corporations to do something meaningful with their work. More and more people are choosing professions primarily based on passion, with salary a secondary consideration. According to a recent *New York Times* article, baby boomers contemplating a career shift are considering fulfillment to be a more pressing job requirement than ever. When Miriam Katowitz was asked why she traded in stock options and professional prestige for her less glamorous position at the 92nd Street Y in Manhattan, she illustrated the above point. "The 92nd Street Y is full of vibrance; you walk into the building and the place hums," Katowitz said. "It's a place that I could feel passionate about."

I'm not saying that money is unimportant. It's still one of the most significant measures of success. And I like having a roof over my head, buying cute shoes, and feeding my children just as much as the next person. Nor am I arguing that being well paid correlates with a lack of productivity; some extraordinarily well-compensated folks have arguably earned their billions and then some. But even

business superstars such as Steve Jobs and Bill Gates have publicly stated that they do what they do, not to get rich and richer, but because they love it. They don't keep working twenty-hour days just to make another billion. They strive to be pioneers, to transform their industries, to create new standards, to help their customers achieve their goals . . . and to have fun. People who take pride in what they do—and it doesn't matter if they're working on auto assembly lines or saving orphans—produce better results.

The problem is that many companies don't realize or acknowledge this. They're shortchanging their people and their productivity by believing (and behaving as if) money is everyone's primary driver. I realize that the obsession with financial reward is hardwired into for-profit organizations—they are, after all, *for-profit* organizations—and I'm certainly not advocating that we abolish them. I'm proposing that corporations broaden their rewards and their understanding of compensation in a number of different directions so that people are more deeply and fully motivated to excel.

Not-for-profits, out of necessity, have learned how to capitalize on the range of meanings that inspire people to work effectively. Most of us simply don't have the resources to wave big fat salaries at our staffs. There are, as usual, some remarkable exceptions. Consider the $120 million that Dick Grasso pocketed while running the (then) not-for-profit New York Stock Exchange or the $12 million salary of Roger Goodell, the commissioner (essentially the CEO) of the NFL. (Yes, the NFL is technically a not-for-profit organization.) No legal or ethical code says that we can't pay big salaries or big bonuses. In fact, the Grasso case reaffirmed that the standard for not-for-profit remuneration is set by the board of directors based on comparable worth. The courts let Dick Grasso keep that pile of money because his board of directors determined it was fair value. However, most boards of directors (and donors) frown upon bloated compensation packages, preferring that the funds be used for program expenses. Consequently, not-for-profit companies typically pay more modest packages to their people. They must lure employees to jobs imbued with meaning and fulfillment. Not-for-

profit employees are just as qualified and passionate as for-profit folks. In fact, what's the toughest job to get right now out of an Ivy League school? A spot with Teach For America. The pay is miserably low, yet the job is so coveted that in 2009 the organization accepted fewer than 10 percent of applicants.

But at least the Teach For America corps members are paid something! Much of the not-for-profit labor force is unpaid. That's right. Nada. Nothing. Zilch. Managing these volunteers is truly a challenge. How do you motivate great people if you don't have financial incentives to dangle in front of them like a fabulous dessert at the end of a mediocre meal? And in the case of volunteers, we may not even be able to hang the threat of termination over their heads. Plus, in some circumstances, like Wikipedia's gigantic volunteer labor force, the organization doesn't select its volunteers; they select us. Imagine if a for-profit company had to hire every single person who asked for a job—and then couldn't use either money or the threat of termination to motivate them. That's what we face.

How do we do it? How do we extract the best from our people, if both the threat of less and the promise of more money is taken off the table? The key to successfully doing more with your people with less money is figuring out what really makes your employees get out of bed in the morning . . . and then giving them more of it.

PRODUCE A HIGH-QUALITY PRODUCT OR SERVICE.

Don't ever underestimate the power of believing in something. People want to work on a product or service that they love and respect. John Lilly, CEO of Mozilla Firefox, the organization dedicated to producing and maintaining an open Internet, likes to talk about how his product "doesn't suck." (That is a direct quote.) Lilly believes that people may try Firefox the first time because of its open philosophy and not-for-profit status, but they keep using it because the product is good. Similarly, the employees and volunteers who work on Firefox upgrades are enthusiastic about delivering the most

accessible form of Internet to the most comprehensive population. The Mozilla team believes in their product, kind of like the way a religious flock has faith in their principles. John says that his employees are looking for the chance to be innovative and participatory. The fervor is born from each employee's clarity and conviction that his or her personal seed will yield a pregnant harvest. The specific product itself is something that makes his people proud.

Especially because for-profits may not offer the same noble purpose as not-for-profits, execs and managers need to cultivate internal enthusiasm for the product or service. Recognize that most people were originally drawn to your field because your product speaks to them in some way. They *chose* the field of advertising or making clothing or selling soap. The next step for an employer is capitalizing on and maintaining that interest. It is crucial to keep people passionate about the purpose. Your employees came to work for you at PricewaterhouseCoopers because they were interested in working as accountants. They've stayed because they believe PwC offers a top-quality service to its clients. People will even take a pay cut to work for a product or service that they're proud to help create.

Does your company focus solely on quarterly numbers, departmental goals, and the stock price? Is that an inspiring place to work? That focus probably encourages your employees to calculate their self-worth in terms of numbers too—that is, the pay package. Instead, focus your team on the quality of what they are creating. People want to work for a product or service that they'd be proud to bring home to Mom.

CREATE A BIG LOFTY PURPOSE—BIG, NOT NECESSARILY CAUSE-Y.

Some people join not-for-profit organizations because they're looking for fulfillment. But fulfillment can take many shapes. Some people are naturally inclined to altruism; they may be looking to save the whales or eliminate illiteracy or shelter the homeless. How-

ever, another fierce motivating force is the desire to be part of something big—something bigger than yourself. In fact, while altruism may be the bait that attracts not-for-profit employees, being part of something big is the hook that retains them. People may join not-for-profits because of our noble goals, but most won't stay with us or work at a high level unless they're getting more out of it than a vague notion of goodness. They want to be part of something big and important—like the Mozilla employees creating more than just a great search engine, but an open Internet. That's a big idea!

Businesses across the board should be cognizant of this "bigger than me" concept. Employees want to work toward a goal that is immodest and broad, regardless of what it is. A not-for-profit employee may thrive on the fact that he is working to combat global hunger, an epidemic that reaches far beyond his city and into all corners of the Earth. That person is imbued with a sense of purpose: *What I do matters to the world.* By the same token, an employee working on a shampoo product can feel the same excitement about her work, which is equally universal and pertinent. You can provide a sense of purpose through the internal dialogue you construct about your company. Instead of selling a lot of shampoo or "the leading shampoo," give your product a purpose, such as washing half the heads in Brazil. It doesn't have to be noble to be inspirational. Being BIG can also be a source of pride. Size leaves people feeling empowered and consequently more productive.

Adam Sterling is the leader of the Sudan Divestment Task Force, which works to orchestrate divestments from Sudan because of the genocide in Darfur. His career illustrates the appeal of working on something big and lofty. At UCLA, Sterling was enrolled in a course on Rwanda, which sparked his interest in genocides. He and his friends were horrified by the stories, the mass destruction, and the fact that very few people were actively trying to stop the genocide. They decided the issue was too big and important to ignore. He and his friends were "just kids"—without contacts or titles or an organization—but they felt compelled to act because they perceived fighting genocide to be important, significant. He and his friends

hosted awareness-building events about Darfur and launched a letter-writing campaign to members of Congress. To date they have successfully convinced six countries and ten companies to divest their investments from Sudan until the genocide stops. Adam and his friends were compensated poorly, if at all, but they knew that their actions were helping to curb the slaughter of actual people.

You can be part of something big too, even if you're not saving lives or the planet. My point is that a company can position its purpose as something meaningful to its employees and make them excited about the actual function of the product or service. For example, the accountants at PwC care that the numbers they crunch be correct, because that is part of creating stronger clients. The product's integrity matters in a meaningful way—even if that meaning is different for each employee.

I am absolutely not suggesting that you place inspirational quote posters on the walls as a means of creating a big, lofty purpose! In fact, show me an office with a wall of posters of soaring eagles and pretty sunsets, and I'll show you employees who are cynical and unproductive. (Think the offices of *Dilbert* and Dunder Mifflin in *The Office.*) These posters and empty statements from management are examples of lip service, and employees can see through them in a second.

I'm also not suggesting that you make donations or support a cause with corporate proceeds as a way to bring meaning to your company. It's great to donate to or support good causes. But these actions won't turn bored, uninspired employees into dynamos. Most of the time the boss picks his or her pet charity, and that's where the money goes—and sometimes the employees feel pressured to support that same group. Yikes. This is not a positive source of motivation. This is a lazy attempt to find meaning by shifting the burden to a third party.

The employees of Estée Lauder should believe that makeup makes women feel powerful and confident. The people behind Six Flags Great Adventure should feel they are part of bringing happiness and excitement to people's lives. And the makers of Purell, the

hand-purification goop, should rest well at night knowing that their company's product is stemming germs and disease. These are all truly wonderful corporate purposes. People will do more work for less money if they work at a place with a clear, lofty purpose.

INCLUDE EVERY LEVEL OF THE COMPANY IN THE PURSUIT OF YOUR PURPOSE.

One day when President Lyndon Johnson was visiting NASA headquarters, he passed by a custodian. Although the president was there to meet with VIP personnel, the two shared a short encounter. "I helped put a man on the moon," relayed the custodian. He did not discuss his individual job; nor did he once mention brooms or emptying waste bins. Because, to the custodian, his purpose transcended these daily janitorial tasks. Yes, even your janitor is part of the pursuit of your corporate purpose.

Some for-profit corporations are secretive with their employees about new products or feel that understanding certain corporate services is irrelevant to those below a certain level. Or they simply aren't interested in taking the time to communicate about those products and services clearly and consistently.

If an organization exudes a fortified brand, its employees will subscribe to a uniform focus at every level and embody a strong sense of purpose that reminds them of their long-term impact and inspires them to be part of it. Most domestic violence shelter employees—down to the bookkeepers and cafeteria workers—know the statistics about domestic violence. In schools, not just the after-school counselors but people at every level know why it's important to keep kids off the streets. For-profit businesses should emulate the not-for-profit sector's ability to consistently imbue staff at every organizational level with a clear sense of purpose and a belief that their individual actions will help realize the overall goal. The resulting passion, poise, and accountability would benefit any and all businesses.

This is especially important for companies with offices in multiple locations. The Make-A-Wish Foundation has nearly one hundred offices around the globe. The kids they help are terminally and chronically ill, with a wide array of illnesses. Not surprisingly, those kids have hugely diverse wish requests. Yet every employee and volunteer at every level of the organization, from Phoenix to Tokyo to Buenos Aires, is focused on the same united purpose: granting more wishes.

Not-for-profits typically do not distribute information in a hierarchical way. Simply put, we're sharers. Nothing is more enervating, as an employee, than sensing you're not in the know, that you're purposely being excluded or even deceived by organizational leaders. It breeds disillusionment and distrust.

Imagine if the support staff at Bank of America better understood the services that the bank offers. Right now most of its employees think of the company as "helping rich people make more money." But what if the bank offered the support staff free evening classes, teaching them basic principles of finance and showing them how their work fits into these principles? Would they not be better at their jobs? Would they be more supportive of their co-workers? Would they have aspirations and dreams to achieve more?

There are various ways to make sure that transparency reaches the lower ranks. New York's Lincoln Center for the Performing Arts is dedicated to providing a space for artistic performances in the heart of Manhattan. One way they do it is to make sure their employees see the fruits of their labor. When your job description includes crunching numbers or pouring coffee, the larger purpose of your work isn't smack in front of your face. Lincoln Center gets those people out from behind their desks to witness a performance, providing them with tickets and event passes. It is important for employees to see that they are part of a decision-making process that leads to something, and that their thoughts are not only valuable but incredibly influential. When an employee who works on the playbill, for example, can see the fruits of his labor in the hands of an actual audience member, his important role in the organiza-

tion becomes real. That employee goes home feeling not only more cultured but also more empowered in his work. And he comes back to the office tomorrow, supermotivated.

Flattening organizations is a step in the right direction, but it isn't the whole answer. Many so-called flat organizations provide a lot of insincere offers of participatory decision-making, but when important decisions must be made (and especially when they must be made quickly), they revert to old-style top-down modes. The not-for-profit model is to find different ways to include more people in the decision-making process as well as keep people aware of what's happening as a decision is discussed and then implemented. I err on the side of bringing too many people into a meeting rather than too few; I also have new hires "shadow" me so they're at least aware of the decision-making process, the key partners, and our quirks.

It's not just a learning opportunity. When people feel they're working *with* others rather than *for* them, they find that work more meaningful. A good litmus test for how well informed employees are is whether they are surprised by shifts in decisions and directions. The less surprised they are, the more they feel they're part of the decision-making process.

In my experience I have always found that you get more with an open hand than with a closed fist. It is important to involve your people in the decision-making process. The not-for-profit world has learned that in doing so, you get more than you give.

CREATE A PHYSICAL WORK ENVIRONMENT THAT STIMULATES YOUR PEOPLE.

A company's offices should reflect who they really are. The walls of my office are made of glass. VolunteerMatch and Idealist.org have open floor plans. That's right. Almost no walls at all. The walls of Citizen Schools' headquarters in Boston are Plexiglas garage doors, so the entire wall moves up into the ceiling with the push of a button! This construction isn't for aesthetics; it's a symbol of

transparency. I ask new hires to sit in the bullpen outside my office for at least three months, so they can listen in on decision-making meetings and learn by proximity. It is a speedy way to expose a new employee to every aspect of the company. While I'm not suggesting that every CEO erect glass-enclosed offices or that every office have a bullpen in the middle, I am advocating fewer closed-door meetings, fewer for-your-eyes-only memos, and fewer executive retreats. And I absolutely think the C-suite concept, that executives should work in a space separate from their employees, is destructive to communication flows.

Too often corporate offices are slickly designed but impersonal spaces. They don't communicate what an organization is all about, either to employees or to visitors. By contrast, not-for-profits rarely have too much space. More often we are squished into tiny spaces, or we outgrow a building and figure out a way to "make it work." And (most of the time) it does. "Working tight" not only is cheaper but also fosters teamwork, shared knowledge, and camaraderie. And like a cook in a kitchen without enough cabinet space, we're forced to focus on what is essential: *Do we have bowls, plates, and cups?*

Too often corporations see bigger as better. They give people perks, such as their own offices or bigger offices. They attempt to spread people out over a large area so they're not on top of one another. What they fail to see is that this policy encourages segregation and isolation. Separating employees by work levels (the executive floor) or by functions (the graphics department) makes it difficult for people to feel like they're all in it together. I'm for communal work spaces and for integrating employees who have different functions and responsibilities.

Charity: water's offices, for example, could be confused for a small college dorm room. The organization strives to provide clean and safe drinking water to the 1.6 billion people on the planet in need of it. Thanks to a noisy industrial neighbor, a rhythmic pounding reverberates through the windowless space, and it's always bustling with "too many" people. But this situation isn't a source of resentment for the staff. According to founder and CEO Scott Har-

rison, its physical space reflects its priorities: to spend money on building wells. "That's why we are here," he says.

In what sounds like the beginning of a bad joke, a construction worker and a financial analyst walk into a room. The encounter ends not with a corny punch line and a stale laugh but in productivity. It's a typical day at Lincoln Center. The finance office isn't a group of cloaked men quietly tinkering on calculators in the basement. Instead, it is the hub of many of Lincoln Center's other dealings, from programming to construction. This "everyone in it together" philosophy means celebrating diversity of experience and skill set.

The not-for-profit world faces monetary strains that limit rent budgets and create physically constrained spaces. But these small places become arenas of diversity and powerhouses of creativity and teamwork. Space constriction should not be lamented for its crowdedness, but celebrated for its multifariousness.

A space can be nurturing and inspirational because of its shape, because there is music, or because the walls are painted a certain color. People can be motivated based on where they sit, who they sit next to, and how office conversation flows. Conversely, unimaginative cubicles are like blinders on a horse, focusing them to keep their heads down and walk only where the master guides them. Is this what we want from a workforce?

Whether you intend it or not, your company's work environment could be limiting your productivity, morale, and consequent future at the company. Conversely, it could be a source of inspiration, comfort, and joy, a place where you envision working for years to come.

NEVER UNDERESTIMATE THE IMPORTANCE OF FUN.

Why do so many organizations approach work with the seriousness of an undertaker? Some corporations, in fact, replicate a high-school algebra-class environment, where talking during class, snacking at desks, and loud laughing are not permitted. All these restrictions

create an oppressive atmosphere that robs people of satisfaction, even when they're doing meaningful work! Completing the assignment becomes the only thing that matters, and that assignment quickly grows onerous.

Yes, at times work is serious business, and treating it frivolously can have negative consequences. Many corporate offices, however, would benefit greatly if they lightened up. Numerous options exist for increasing the fun quotient of an office—and I'm not talking about bringing in cereal dispensers and a foosball table. At DoSomething.org, for example, we've turned Valentine's Day into an official holiday. I want everyone at my office to have a little love in his or her life—even if that special person is Mom. I think it's important that our company provides one day a year for love! We also have an office kickball team, which costs us nothing. We didn't join a league; instead, we send out challenges to companies we want to get to know. What self-respecting person would turn down a game of kickball?

Rodrigo Mendes runs an institute in Brazil that uses art to mentor disabled youths. Many of his employees are artists, so he gives them access to supplies and provides them with creative time. He even lets them bring their children to the classes they teach, a nice perk for people who are interested in art and likely want to expose their children to it. Cost to him and his org? Zilch.

Here is a simple truism that companies should keep in mind: the more fun work is, the more willing people are to go to work. The companies that complain that their people are just going through the motions or aren't committed to company goals are generally ones that treat work with the seriousness of dentistry. Fun, on the other hand, fosters involvement and excitement, a willingness to try new things, and a desire to focus on the work rather than watch the clock.

People are attracted to happy work environments, and they stay there. Darell Hammond is the founder and CEO of KaBOOM!— an organization that builds playgrounds in underprivileged areas across the country. Beyond his impressive work with low-income

communities, he has successfully created an enticing package for his employees. The organization celebrates every employee's birthday in a meaningful way, and it holds a monthly Peanut Butter & Jelly Day, where employees enjoy a sponsored lunch of peanut butter and jelly sandwiches. As small as these gestures may seem, their existence "redefines what's in it for them," the employees. A birthday cake is a small perk, but celebrating with a second family is a big perk.

A million opportunities exist to make work fun, ranging from providing employees with rooms where they can play Ping-Pong, pool, and video games, to offering them use of exercise facilities, to scheduling events like free movies, book clubs, and potluck lunches throughout the day. My office has very silly bake-off competitions. One day employees are challenged to make "something square" and another day it may be "something that includes fruit." These noncompulsory team-building activities cost us nothing but add laughter and camaraderie.

OFFER SKILL DEVELOPMENT.

What could be more valuable than helping employees develop new skills or acquire new knowledge? Skills translate to greater career success, either in your organization or somewhere else. In a world that is increasingly knowledge-driven, the chance to acquire expertise in a critical area can make a huge difference in an individual's career. Not-for-profits possess numerous options to help their people acquire skills and knowledge, from providing in-house classes to paying for seminar and workshop tuition. Some have formal job-switching or apprenticeship programs. People are keenly aware that knowledge and skills are the foundation of great careers, and having the chance to acquire some of both can make even a mundane job meaningful.

In my office I have created a kind of guest mentoring program. Periodically I bring in thought-leaders and innovators for one-on-

one sessions with my people. The other day, for example, Caterina Fake, founder of Flickr, the first and largest photo-sharing website (it was purchased by Yahoo in March 2005), spent about an hour sitting with my chief technology officer, getting to know him and offering thoughts on our website-redesign plans. Georges Harik, one of the first dozen Google employees and the guy who led the team that created Gmail, has also spent some time in our offices mentoring our CTO. Recently our two content writers spent an afternoon at the CNN offices, with a Pulitzer Prize–winning producer. No specific agenda, just the chance to share experiences and ask questions. Not-for-profits know how to reach out to experts, not just to make our organizations stronger but also to facilitate our people's growth. Nearly a dozen thought-leaders have come through my offices, spent unstructured time getting to know our people and programs, and offered advice. It's a terrific priceless perk.

For-profit companies bring in big-name speakers or entertainers (usually at a high cost). But do these people spend time in a small format with anyone other than senior executives? Tell Jimmy Buffett to leave the guitar at home. Instead of entertaining the Time Warner holiday party, wouldn't it be more useful for him to spend an hour getting to know the editorial staff, explaining his creative process, and exchanging best practices on writer's block?

DOLE OUT TITLES LIBERALLY.

People often define themselves by their job titles, and it costs nothing to give them a title that suits them and makes them proud. Most for-profits tend to rely on a stock group of titles. You are a product associate and then a manager and then a director of product and eventually (you hope) an EVP of product. There's nothing wrong with these titles, and they are exactly how some people want to define themselves. People aspire to the higher title, so why not give it to them? You can confer vice president status on people without spending a dime.

Better yet, you can make up a new title that makes employees feel valued. Is that person really a communications manager or is he the Manager of Buzz? Jerry Yang was famously not the CEO of Yahoo but rather the Chief Yahoo. The title itself can inspire people to think differently, think bigger, or feel appreciated. I've given business cards and titles to interns and volunteers—and it is amazing to see them network a room with pride and hold their heads just a little bit higher.

Of course, if you give everyone a title, the importance is diluted. A title has to reflect an employee's talent and worth, not just the employer's appreciation. So give a fitting title. Spend ten minutes crafting something relevant and appropriate. Not-for-profits have discovered that people often view themselves in highly specialized and sometimes idiosyncratic ways. For this reason, one employee may prefer to be called Head Donor Strategist or Innovation Specialist or Team Builder. My title is actually "CEO and Chief Old Person," and I appreciate the humor in it, which sets the tone for our office culture. Titles offer people a sense of identity in the workplace, and finding the right one (and not being locked into traditional titles) is worth the effort.

One not-for-profit friend of mine thinks that a title's tangible representation is even more meaningful. Having the title emblazoned on an office name plaque or even creating an award that explains it can be significant to people. Not only does it remind them that they have been recognized for their contributions and knowledge, it communicates their worth to others. As people enter an office, they can refer to the plaque to orient themselves and pick up on the tone of the office.

REMEMBER THAT ACCOMPLISHING GOALS FEELS PRICELESSLY GOOD.

I have two employees who are semiprofessional long-distance runners. Some have difficulty appreciating the mind-set of people who

run just for the sake of running—not to put a ball in the end zone or to train for a tennis match. These guys simply love to set goals and achieve them. At work, not surprisingly, they are motivated by the same quantifiable goal-setting.

Some people like being able to see a number on the horizon—and then overshooting that goal. It makes them feel good or useful, part of a team, even if that number is meaningless to the overall organizational purpose or any other team member.

Some people are achievement junkies and need to push themselves to the next level, like running an under-four-minute mile. So set a goal for them, and then help them achieve it. To such people, it's more satisfying than receiving a financial bonus at the end of the quarter.

But asking my long-distance runners to run an under-three-minute mile wouldn't make much sense. That just isn't possible. Instead, we set attainable goals—not too easy, but not too hard either.

Some people like setting their own goals. Instead of handing down a quarterly sales target, try asking the sales team to help set it. Clearly there are limits in this area, since the organization needs each employee to contribute to the greater whole (in theory, at least). You can't have someone in finance ignoring his financial responsibilities because he wants to spend time developing a new product introduction.

When a company dictates exactly what an employee should do, personal gain is hard to come by; again, this is an example of working-for rather than working-with. Not-for-profit executives have to be more flexible. Often the employee in the field first senses the market shift.

Do your employees know the overall corporate goal and their role in achieving it? If so, it's easier for them to create benchmarks for themselves. Does the company listen to employees' concerns about market and technology constraints? If so, it's easier for the company to create realistic overall goals that take into account what the employees can actually execute. Simply put, goal-setting isn't a

negotiation that results in a happy medium; it should be a conversation that leads to productive decision-making.

CREATE NONWORK WORK TIME.

Every organization participates in events outside the office, which are integral to what the company is all about. They can range from trade shows to sponsored promotional events to market weeks. Participating in these activities can be tremendously fulfilling for your employees, who can get out of the office and become involved in the organization in galvanizing ways. Employees often love working booths at trade shows or attending annual conferences. Too often, though, for-profits limit participation to a select few, and the majority of employees never get to experience this active involvement.

In fact, trade shows are a terrific way to initiate newbies. It conveys your confidence in them as ambassadors. It gives them a reason to double-down on their knowledge of the company. And it gives them a chance to bond with veterans.

Can you rotate which employees attend NASCAR races to make sure that your logo is on the car and you are receiving your perks? Take the M&M car, for example—is it always Mars's senior executives at the track? Has Mars considered rotating the privilege to the drivers who deliver the candies or to the executive assistants who provide much of the company's administrative backbone? What a perk! What a nice way to appreciate people! And it might make them a better ambassador for the brand or stir their creative juices to think of ways to maximize the partnership in their corner of the company.

Notice that I'm not necessarily suggesting a one-day, once-a-year event. Corporations are notorious for setting aside one day to do something they believe employees will find meaningful and then hoping the effect lasts all year. They have a one-day blood drive or a summer picnic. These are token efforts. Removing people from the workplace suggests that the only way to build a team is to "get the

heck outta the office." Instead, have that nonoffice time be work-related. You are trying to foster work relationships, not personal relationships or hot-dog-eating skills.

CELEBRATE THE CREATIVITY AND ENERGY OF YOUNG PEOPLE.

One way to look at the conundrum of maximizing cheap labor is to examine the management of millennials. Most high-performing not-for-profits have figured out how to utilize young, hungry, cheap labor. A lot has been written about managing the generation born between 1980 and 1990. According to Ron Alsop, author of *The Trophy Kids Grow Up*, this generation has grown up in the age of e-mail, texting, Facebook, and Twitter. Big business could stand to learn from the way many not-for-profits are harnessing this generation's energy and knowledge and directing it toward specific goals.

The millennial generation comprises a significant percentage of the not-for-profit workforce, and savvy leaders know that these young people have certain requirements and preferences, which we make an effort to satisfy. Not-for-profits don't necessarily create formal programs to do so, but we take informal steps to make sure that the work remains meaningful for the younger people on staff.

For instance, Heidrick and Struggles' statistics show that, on average, millennials will have fourteen jobs before age forty. At the mention of a more promising job, they are likely to bolt. They get bored quickly. They believe they have mastered their job in about six months. They want new challenges. Basically, they live their work life as if they were trapped inside a video game: fast, goal-oriented, expecting to accrue points, with do-overs.

How do you get the most out of someone who seems to live in a virtual world? By recognizing that what they long for (and are often denied) is real responsibility. Many of the not-for-profit heads I've interviewed use responsibility as a perk, entrusting these people with important assignments. They offer young people the

opportunity to take on critical tasks and to use their ingenuity and resources to complete them successfully. VolunteerMatch, which is based in San Francisco, has an important outpost in Washington, D.C., charged with overseeing the organization's relationships with the White House and the National Corporation for Community Service, as well as coordinating with other large national not-for-profits, pushing for legislative policies that might affect volunteer-ism, and procuring public funds. As I write these words, that office is led by one woman who only recently turned thirty. And she rocks it. She relishes the responsibility. Conscious of the assumptions that will be made about her based on her age, she always wears a crisp suit, arrives on time, and sends a formal e-mail after meetings. Basi-cally, she overcompensates for her perceived handicap and inevita-bly winds up being the most mature and professional person in the room. Simply put, that ambitious millennial feeds off responsibility, as the rest of us need food and water.

Many corporations give people responsibility based on senior-ity; they have paid their dues and demonstrated they are worthy of decision-making authority or working on certain projects. Millen-nials bring a fresh outlook to problem-solving. They hear the words "It's always been done that way" and see that as a challenge. Tradi-tion isn't something to respect, it's an opportunity for improvement. Trying to change these ambitious kids to meet your corporate cul-ture is as good as walking them to the nearest exit. But harnessing this ambition is like tapping into a new fuel source.

Giving young people responsibility isn't a panacea, of course; we also need to be clear about what success looks like. Often, in for-profit companies, specific goals are articulated ("complete the task"), but measures of success aren't. No one is quite clear what constitutes the successful completion of an assignment—such a de-termination is made only after the assignment is completed.

This approach doesn't work for millennials. They need a clear explanation of when the project is due, what they have to accom-plish, what will happen if they achieve their goal successfully, and so on. Don't just tell them what to do, tell them why it matters.

Tell them the pain points you're trying to eliminate. For example, instead of "I need you to lead the project to overhaul the packaging design, and it is due next week," sit down and explain what would make this redesign a success. Specifically, identify who will be evaluating this project and what their needs are. Millennials want approval. When success is defined for them in advance, they go after the goal like tigers. They're energized not just by the responsibility for an important project but by the clarity of a successful outcome.

I use millennials as an example here because my corporate brethren complain that their young people are lazy; that they don't stay with the company for long; they aren't team players; they don't like too much supervision; and they don't take responsibility. The problem, of course, is that you can't motivate someone who wants everything now the same way you motivate someone who wants everything gradually. Not-for-profits don't complain that young people are inherently lazy or unmotivated. Instead, we rely on young people as a major source of labor because they come cheap and they bring passion. We've found that they're tremendous contributors, but it's up to management to figure out how to inspire them to contribute.

SAY THANK YOU. (REALLY. IT'S THAT SIMPLE. AND IT'S FREE.)

People want to know that the leadership of a company values their contribution. Sure, some organizations distribute little buttons or recognize employees by name in a newsletter. These things don't cost much money and may be a valued form of support for some people.

I'm actually thinking of something far more basic and less expensive: a good old-fashioned, personal "thank you." When the right person gives an employee that heartfelt message, be it face-to-face or in a handwritten note or a voicemail message, it can motivate the person for months.

One of my employees, Melanie, brought in three important new partnerships in the last two months and is beating all her quarterly goals. She doesn't report to me, but I'm aware of her success. I sent her an e-mail telling her that I'm impressed by what she has been achieving lately and how grateful I am to have her on our team. Ever since Melanie received this note, she has spoken up in staff meetings with greater confidence. And last week she even stuck her head into my office to present a new idea. Would a financial raise have had the same effect? Maybe. But it sets a different expectation for her future contributions—and those of her colleagues. And frankly, giving money costs money. Saying thank you costs nothing but my own ability to show gratitude.

REVIEW YOUR PEOPLE, NOT JUST THEIR JOBS.

Corporations routinely conduct performance reviews, but some of the not-for-profit leaders I've spoken to integrate personal objectives into these reviews. Thinking of your people as human beings, not just as employees, changes the dynamic of the review process. It's no longer just about being judged but about a mutual exchange of meaningful information. Rodrigo Mendes of the Rodrigo Mendes Institute in Brazil said to me, "Employees are people first, workers second." They have hopes and dreams, problems and concerns. To ignore them is to communicate that their hopes, dreams, problems, and concerns don't matter to the organization. This is a sure way to alienate people emotionally. Do you want mercenaries in your workplace?

Instead, try to find the answers to the following questions during a quarterly review:

- ☐ What is your consuming passion during your nonwork hours? Are you doing it?

- ☐ Have you made time for fun recently?

☐ Is there something you want to learn?

☐ Are you planning some life-changing event during the next quarter—getting married, buying your first house?

☐ Where do you want to be in five years?

☐ What will your tombstone read?

Obviously, you need to be conscious of where you're crossing the line and becoming too intrusive. Back off if you sense someone feels you're invading his privacy. Most of the time, though, employees at all levels love to talk about their significant life events and goals. It makes them feel valued in a way that transcends hearing they did a good job on a project. Perhaps even more significant, it allows them to balance their personal and professional lives. When you know that someone is going through a rough patch at home (a divorce, a sick child), you may decide not to burden them with a project that requires a great deal of travel and late hours. If you've established clear communication, you can ask them if they want this additional responsibility right now, giving them an out. Avoiding or completely ignoring these conversations may compound the feelings of frustration that they may already be facing. Knowing that they're a valued team member—and valued human being—can be important during tough personal times. Conversely, if they're at loose ends in their personal life, they may want a meaty project that they can really sink their teeth into. In either case, people are grateful when their bosses accommodate who they are at a given moment with the work they assign them.

Employers benefit too from becoming much more attuned to the moods and requirements of their people. When you start thinking about your direct reports in terms beyond the office, you will have a much better sense of how to treat them. Motivation becomes much easier when you know the whole person, not just the business part. You learn that some people need big challenges while others need smaller ones; that some work best under deadline pressure while others function best with longer time frames. Best of all, your

information from the quarterly personal reviews exists in real time. You're not operating on false assumptions or on information you gathered a few years ago when you first hired them.

Really, these reviews should be seen as a continuation of the interview process. Ask the same kinds of questions (and respect the same legal boundaries). Getting to know your people and making sure the fit is there shouldn't stop the day you hire someone, it should be the beginning of that relationship.

ELEVEN QUESTIONS TO GET YOU STARTED:
Do More with Less Cash to Throw at People

Managing volunteers and/or very poorly paid people (without hope of a salary increase or bonus) is an art form. It's like showing up to a boxing match without arms. What you thought was your biggest, most obvious weapon in the fight to motivate simply doesn't exist. But we in the not-for-profit world know that it's possible to inspire and fulfill your employees without fat paychecks. We find other incentives to compensate their time, energy, ideas, and accomplishments.

Think about a group in your organization that you're particularly concerned about. It may not be age-related but have to do with function (say, a group of engineers) or country (an office elsewhere). Now ask these eleven questions:

1. Are their goals well defined or loosely defined?

2. Who created those goals and how?

3. Is the supervision close or loose?

4. Do your people prefer to be freed from paperwork or to chart their own progress, submitting reports when necessary?

5. When was the last time you thanked them for something big or small that they accomplished, asked, or suggested?

6. When was the last time you saw them smile? I don't mean at a joke or a photo of a co-worker's new grandchild. I mean smile because of something related to work.

7. What is the color of their office walls? Can you even name it? Can you close your eyes and draw a rough floor plan?

8. When was the last time they were out of their office and in the field, interacting with the end user?

9. Are YOU proud of what you make or do? Does it make you feel like an industry leader?

10. What is this group learning right now that is new to them?

11. Do people in this group thrust their business cards into people's hands because they are proud of their title? Do those business titles make sense to you?

DO MORE WITH YOUR BRAND

AT A FORBES CONFERENCE I once listened to Shelly Lazarus, the CEO of Ogilvy & Mather, describe a brand as "360 degrees—every touch a company has with the public." A brand is so much more than the product or the service itself. It's bigger than a logo or a tagline. It's the receptionist's tone of voice when she answers the phone, the experience of every single consumer, a typo in a letter to a donor, the reputation of a celebrity spokesperson, the quality of the programs, and the composition of the board of directors. It is our every action and inaction—the unintended consequences as well as the intended ones. A brand is that big.

Which explains why big companies spend billions of dollars on focus groups, design, storyboards, media planning, media buying, media evaluation, and redesign, right? With all that spending, you would think they'd have bought all the knowledge and wisdom there is about brands. So what can for-profits possibly learn from not-for-profits about creating and maintaining strong brands?

They can learn how to do it well, for zilch.

The terrain between idea and implementation is treacherous and disorienting, and that's where the authenticity of a big fat company gets lost. In many instances, corporate brands and the campaigns to promote them seem impersonal at best and manipulative or deceptive at worst. The underlying themes of these efforts may have made sense when they were articulated to focus groups and in strategy sessions, but the size and scope of the branding process somehow dilutes or distorts the message. A corporation may want to convey how its products are all about helping people live better lives, and it may be true, but the ultimate communication comes across as self-serving and grandiose. Companies invest too much money in creating campaigns that are too slick, too well coordinated; they spend too much time defining and refining the brand position; they involve too many distant people in the process.

Not-for-profits, by contrast, create their brands with little money and even less research. It's not a strategic decision—usually we have no choice because we lack the funds, or we choose to spend our funds on the programs instead. Still, even without huge wads of money to create, maintain, and evaluate our brands, the not-for-profit world has managed to build strong, iconic companies with household names, including Make-A-Wish, Habitat for Humanity, and Teach For America.

You may be wondering why a strong brand is important to a not-for-profit—isn't it all about the cause, not the company? But volunteers, donors, and workers are all attracted to strong brands. An organization that has strong brand recognition and built-in consumer loyalty doesn't need to spend as much on marketing to convey its message, which leads to greater financial efficiency. A strong brand creates a high barrier to entry for competitors. A strong brand produces opportunities to partner with for-profit corporations on cause-marketing campaigns. But perhaps most important, a strong brand is important to a not-for-profit organization because, truly, its brand is its only asset.

Most not-for-profits don't make anything or sell anything or

own anything proprietary. We're in the business of making and selling goodness of some kind. We don't have a secret recipe or a patented process. Our name, our history, our essence—all those intangibles comprise our true worth. Which is why the best of us guard our brands so fiercely.

In 2001 Interbrand, the country's leading brand-valuation agency, assessed the value of Habitat for Humanity's brand at $2 billion. Habitat doesn't own much—not the houses it builds, none of the forklifts or tractors or materials it uses, nor the design process itself. What it does have is enormous global name recognition (with more than two thousand affiliates), affinity, and trust, which it has built with a marketing and communications budget that's ridiculously small compared with a for-profit company of similar prestige and visibility.

How do the best brand managers in the not-for-profit world create strong brands without spending ridiculous amounts of money? What are the tricks of our alchemistic trade? How exactly do you create a billion-dollar brand on a budget of zero?

KEEP IT SIMPLE.

A simple brand is a memorable brand. But simplicity can be a tough challenge for huge organizations, since their size and scale create mind-boggling, often global complexity. It's difficult to keep things simple when you have offices in fifty countries, when you have a hundred thousand employees, when you're in the midst of acquiring twenty companies, and when you're trying to restructure ten business units around the world. Yowza!

The solution is to develop a myopia in which you focus on the core purpose and never lose sight of it. Good not-for-profits don't gunk up their messages with convoluted rationales and multipart platforms. They focus on a core idea and pound it home. With the best not-for-profits, you can summarize what they do and what they stand for in a few words. That's the test of a great but simple brand.

Sometimes brands are simple because the organization sticks with a single programmatic function. For instance, Volunteer Match.org is exactly what it says it is: a website that matches volunteer hands with organizations that need them. With more than sixty thousand not-for-profit organizations as members, it could easily expand its functions beyond connecting orgs with people, to listing job opportunities or providing additional services. Cofounder and CEO Greg Baldwin explained to me that they have thought about those kinds of new products and services but decided instead to delve deeply into one area: "We want to rule the volunteer space." If VolunteerMatch.org became a hub for career searchers, it might be a more helpful website for some, but would people remember it long term or be able to describe it in fifteen seconds when they recommend it to friends? In other words, would it be just as strong a brand?

Similarly, from the beginning Dress for Success was focused exclusively on women; in its early days one board member urged us to expand our services to include dressing men for job interviews. Many of our referral agencies were coed, so potential clients were already in the pipeline. No other program existed to serve this need. The law firms, banks, and other offices where we conducted suit drives were full of men eager to contribute clothing as well as money to the cause. Our board gave the idea careful consideration, but in the end we decided not to complicate the brand. Instead, we happily helped this board member start his own organization, Career Gear, which targeted men. Meanwhile, Dress for Success remained a women's organization—choosing to have a clean, crisp focus and protecting the brand's simplicity.

Simple doesn't necessarily mean small. In fact, simplicity can be a terrific precursor for scale. People in different parts of the country contacted me wanting to open Dress for Success shops in their areas. The question before us was, how should we expand? We considered becoming owner-operators in new markets but decided against it because, as a not-for-profit, why take on new liabilities if there were no profits? On the counsel of some very wise pro bono

advisers from Avon, we opted to use a franchise model instead, because it seemed best suited (pardon the pun) to rapid expansion. Within two years we were dressing women for job interviews in nearly forty markets nationwide. You might expect that we would have growing pains from that kind of ridiculous growth—we certainly did, especially since our application procedures and licensing agreements were quite sophomoric. And yet in large part because of the simplicity of our model, every Dress for Success affiliate from London to Lackawanna was able to stay true to the brand: giving suits to women going to job interviews.

In an ideal world, every for-profit would be able to choose a simple core competency, as VolunteerMatch and Dress for Success did. But the reality of business today is that you can't always do that. Sometimes as a result of following the money in new product opportunities and fast-growing, rapidly evolving sectors, businesses become complicated. But even a complicated business model can have a simple brand.

Consider UNICEF. This sprawling organization has offices in 190 countries, and its New York office alone employs more than one hundred people—it is, after all, part of the UN, which isn't exactly the epitome of efficiency. The UNICEF United States Fund website says that the organization spent nearly $3 billion in 2007 alone. That's big by any standard, but in not-for-profit terms it's a behemoth. In 2007 it did something wise: it tried to pull it all together by asking, *What do we do better than anyone else?* The answer: *We are good at saving children.*

UNICEF committed to working toward a future in which no child is forsaken. That's it. It's hugely complex, yet remarkably simple—and from that realization a new tagline was born: "Believe in zero." It means that zero children die of preventable causes. The idea is to do whatever it takes to save a child. The tagline became a rallying cry, and the staff—with its diverse programs, diverse cultures, diverse locations, and diverse thinking—were united and emboldened by UNICEF's singularly focused brand. One number, echoed across the globe by every employee in every office: zero.

I sometimes refer to simplicity as "The FedEx Principle." FedEx was a very expensive, very complicated start-up—from the day it launched, it had to be able to deliver packages all over the place, overnight. It's got an enormous fleet of airplanes and all the accompanying hassles, from security to fuel prices to weather to personnel. It is an incredibly seasonal business, expanding and contracting for various holidays, business cycles, and consumer whims. You think it's annoying to have to take off your shoes at the airport security check? Imagine running an airline where all you ship is packages— that you haven't packed. Basically, it's a tough, complicated business. But how does the public think of FedEx? It's the company that gets stuff there overnight. That's all we need to know. That's the simple brand FedEx holds out to us, even if it needs an incredibly complex infrastructure to make it happen.

A big company can have a complicated business or multiple locations and still be held together by a simple concept. Staying loyal to that focus makes your brand stronger—and costs you less money in the long run.

BE UNIQUE.

The save-the-world sector is crowded and competitive. Organizations must ask themselves, "How is our breast cancer group different from the dozen other breast cancer groups?" The trick is to be able to use one or more of the following terms to describe your organization: *first, only, faster, better, cheaper*. I call these "The Five." (Why? Because giving it a name—even a dumb name like The Five—makes it far easier to remember that there are five key words.) So long as you can pin yourself to one of these words, you've found a niche.

Vartana was created by Aaron Pereira three years ago as Canada's "first financial institution committed to serving the needs of the voluntary sector." Before Vartana, Canadian not-for-profits found it hard to convince banks to give them loans. This was a huge prob-

lem; the growth of the Canadian not-for-profit sector was being stunted by its lack of access to credit or financing. Vartana was the first to solve this problem, creating new lending and borrowing possibilities for banks and not-for-profits. They pioneered a new business, demonstrating that investing with a not-for-profit can be safe and lucrative.

Did you pay attention when you heard the word *first*? This is Vartana's hook. It makes it special, and it helps you remember why Vartana matters and what it does. Because it was the *first* to do it.

New York Road Runners is the only organization that organizes races for runners living in New York City. Anytime a runner is interested in racing, or anytime a runner is looking for training tips, he or she has *only* one place to turn. NYRR has carved out its niche as the center for all running needs in the city. It owns a market. The brand stands alone, recognizable and ready for runners, sponsors, and volunteers.

Ask yourself: Wouldn't it be dreamy if your company were the *only* something? Or, could it lay claim to the *first* moniker?

Maybe *first* and *only* aren't possible for your company. But are you faster, better, or cheaper? Doctors Without Borders, which is headquartered in Switzerland, has an unyielding commitment to being the fastest on arrival when medical help is needed. Its unbounded dedication to reaching a crisis zone quickly, despite all the geographic hurdles and bureaucratic obstacles, is what earns the organization renown and respect. They're medical magicians, spiriting themselves to places of greatest need. And donors return to the brand because they know that Doctors Without Borders will make good use of donated funds by being the *fastest* medics on the scene.

Many markets are incredibly crowded, but that shouldn't be an insurmountable obstacle. The right business can still climb to the top of the heap. Take the online job-search business. There are gazillions of job-search websites, including the formidable for-profit giants Monster and Yahoo! HotJobs. But Idealist.org is the *best* for not-for-profit searches. It has the largest number of listings. It's easy to navigate. And it has the best international searches, with over

ninety thousand organizations from one hundred eighty countries listing on the site. It's the best.

Sometimes the differentiator is that the organization provides a product or service more affordably than anyone else. Craigslist is u-g-l-y, *ugly*. It will never win a prize for beautiful design. Nobody goes there to admire its elegance. I defy you to find a single frill on that gigantic site. So why do more than 10 million people visit the site each month? Because if you want to buy a car or find a roommate, it's the cheapest way to do it. It's hard to beat free. We remember craigslist and love it—and most important, we use it—because of that distinction. Its unique value proposition is that it's free. God bless Craig and his list.

For-profit companies can find their uniqueness too. For some reason, ice cream companies are actually very good at finding ways to be unique. Häagen-Dazs is the rich, luxurious option in the supermarket freezer case, thanks to its gold-laced packaging and Park Avenue–esque flavor names. Ben & Jerry's occupies the crunchy yet upscale and slightly funky slot, with groovy flavor combinations, generous chunks, and goofy packaging. Cold Stone Creamery is the only major chain to offer mix-ins on a cold stone slab while the staff sings silly songs for tips. Carvel was the first to sell soft serve (and dip). And in the early days, Baskin-Robbins was the first place that offered thirty-one flavors, and now it's the cheapest.

They all offer delicious, creamy love in a cup or cone, and yet these brands are distinct. Each is unique because each has found at least one of the five to hang its hat on: *first, only, faster, better, cheaper.* We know their differences practically by heart, which shows us that they've all been quite successful at brand development over the years.

BE CONSISTENT.

In the fall of 2008, possibly the most ubiquitous word in the news was *change*. Change in Washington. Change in politics. Change in society. Change in the way we do business. Ch-ch-ch-ch-ch-

changes! It was as if a 1972 David Bowie had hijacked the message machines of America. The voters seemed to be enthralled with the idea of it—and change is good, right?

Well, not necessarily. Society may be superficially infatuated with novelty and change, but when it comes to branding, consistency is paramount. Consumers have expectations of packaging, of taste, of price point, and so on. Think of the Coke/New Coke debacle, or the recent Tropicana new-packaging backlash. Fall short of those expectations, and you may do worse than disappoint consumers— you may lose them forever. You have to stay faithful to them.

I'm not advocating mindless rigidity. No doubt organizations have to be flexible to respond to changing markets. And I'm certainly not opposed to adapting a company's structure or products to new realities. For example, DoSomething.org had offices in twenty cities throughout the United States. Then came the explosion of the Internet—that's where kids started spending their time. So when I arrived at Do Something in 2003 (the year after Friendster, the year before Facebook), I told the board that I was shutting down the local offices and putting the entire thing online. It was bigger than just adding the ".org" to our name; this was a huge operational departure. But we were loyal to our customer and dedicated to young people leading social change. Shifting our distribution channels to adapt to advances in technology and to teen trends reflected the consistency of our teen-centric brand. We resolved to be true to our market.

Brand consistency isn't necessarily about packaging, words, operations, or people. It's qualitative. It's about remembering your essence and focusing on your core. Every Dress for Success affiliate in more than a hundred cities in eight countries offers suits to women going for job interviews. The volunteers in each outlet are "personal shoppers," which means they treat the clients with more attention than a valet, but with less intrusiveness than a mentor. The clients always come by referral from other NGOs. Are there local variations? Absolutely. In Tampa Bay they distribute far more colorful jackets than in New York. In Texas the big annual fund-raiser involves fly-fishing, while in Boise it's an auction of painted teapots.

But the fundamentals are the same everywhere. That consistent brand—from suits to self-sufficiency—is what the Dress for Success affiliates want from their brand participation. In fact, more than a dozen of the current Dress for Success affiliates once were different organizations, like Suits You San Diego and Tailored Transitions in Denver. But they saw the value of being part of a larger, more recognizable national brand, and so they opted to become part of Dress for Success, which meant adopting the policies that have enabled the brand to become something worth joining.

This consistency is also crucial to the vitality of for-profit brands. A brand has to stand for something, and that something shouldn't be changing constantly. That's how you build the right set of consumer expectations, and that's how you cultivate loyalty.

A word of warning: too often companies use the need for consistency as an excuse for generating a lot of rules and procedures. But the point is to provide a consistent product or service, not to bedevil your employees with the reincarnation of Soviet bureaucracy.

BE RELEVANT TO YOUR AUDIENCE.

It doesn't make much sense to open a pork stand on the streets of Jerusalem or a surf shop in the middle of Nebraska. It's Business 101 to remember the importance of knowing your audience, their preferences, their needs, and their desires. Forget your audience, and you do a disservice to your brand, because ultimately a brand is worthless without someone to want it. But it's Business 102 to learn how to do this without spending oodles of money.

A good brand goes to surprising lengths to be relevant. Lincoln Center is one of the premier places for performing arts excellence in New York, if not the entire country: it has the ballet, the symphony, the opera, and the cachet. The leadership of Lincoln Center recognized that the vast majority of its performances happen just around dinnertime, which was both a business opportunity and a chance to burnish its brand. Lincoln Center's patrons are typically

not Taco Bell or KFC regulars. So Lincoln Center set up an eatery next to the entryway that serves dishes made of "artisanal ingredients," and offers fine wine and parfaits (a fancy-pants way of saying "ice cream sundaes"). Lincoln Center works hard to understand the demographics of its constituents—not just their ages, professions, and addresses but also their eating habits and their shopping preferences. That data colors every decision it makes—from the seasonal programming (of course) to the coffee they serve (hmm . . .) to the fonts on the invitations they send (wow).

How does Lincoln Center do it? Its board members are patrons. As I noted in Chapter 1, the staff members attend performances. And feedback forms are everywhere. In a nutshell? Lincoln Center is listening and watching and learning. In a cluttered cultural market, with shrinking disposable income, it knows that its success depends on sensitivity to its market. It must offer things that make sense for its customers lives, or they will go elsewhere. Sound familiar?

Companies that think carefully about their relevance make decisions based on what they believe their constituents want and need. The consumer-focused lens must be ever present. This doesn't mean living in constant fear of alienating your audience, but rather the inverse: staying relevant and vigilantly pursuing all that you can do to make them happy—and more loyal.

I like that Best Buy, the retailing giant, gets so into the head of its target consumers that it has actually named them. For example, "Jill" is the suburban mom who wants quality at a good price, is concerned about what video games her kids play, and isn't sure she knows as much as she should about the latest trends. Do you know your consumers? Do you know not only what but *who* influences their purchases? And do you know enough about them that you could profile them and talk about them as if they were a family friend or neighbor?

The next level of relevance is less personal and more societal. A brand has to be relevant to the times and responsive to current trends. Losing touch with your target market's pain points isn't an

option—the opposite of relevance is obsolescence, and in the business world, obsolescence means getting ready for the "going out of business" sale.

Recently Madrasati, a Jordanian initiative chaired by Queen Rania, made impressive efforts to take relevance to the next level. It has quickly become one of the largest organizations in the Middle East focusing on social services. Not too long ago I visited a school for deaf children outside Amman that had recently been renovated with Madrasati's support. Each classroom had a beautiful new computer with Internet access and preloaded software for teaching deaf children how to sign and read. The students seemed happy, the teachers engaged.

The conventional path would dictate that Madrasati should keep updating the software, keep supporting the teachers, and keep the entire school going. But then it learned about a way to improve students' learning beyond the classroom, complementing those in-school efforts: using cochlear implants. Statistics show that when children over the age of nine undergo this surgical intervention, within five years 100 percent are able to learn how to read and most are able to speak. The leaders of the school and of Madrasati realized that it would make sense for the program—excellent already—to shift some of its spending toward facilitating cochlear implants for its students. Only by paying assiduous attention to staying relevant did they make this decision. Only through an exquisite understanding of its audience's needs—and its possibilities—was this project able to weigh priorities and to ensure that it made the right choices.

It can be extremely difficult to abandon or change a successful program, product, or service. Companies can be just as sentimental as people. Corporations tend to be risk averse, preferring to keep doing what has worked before. But your loyalty must be to your audience and to your brand, not to your current lineup of products and services. And if your audience's needs can or must be addressed in a new way, then it's up to you to make the changes in your products and services necessary to retain them.

CREATE A WRITTEN SET OF GUIDELINES.

Sometimes a company works to focus its brand into a brilliantly simple, unique, consistent, relevant concept . . . and then two months later, with the launch of a new flavor or the emergence of a new technology, everything changes. People abandon that discipline like a hungry dieter at an all-you-can-eat buffet. Call it the brand-drift binge. Suddenly all the options, so recently off limits, look so darn tasty!

It's worth sitting down and putting on paper exactly what your simple, unique, consistent, relevant brand is. Please don't call it a mission statement. Those corny, vacuous statements might look pretty in a bold typeface on the inside cover of an annual report or painted across the wall of a corporate lobby, but they invite your employees to snicker because those empty words were never truly adopted and never truly meant.

What I'm suggesting is a practical guide, one that your people might actually use.

Nothing But Nets is a United Nations Foundation organization that purchases and distributes insecticide-treated bed nets in the developing world in an effort to eradicate malaria. The organization created a brand binder for its employees, listing all its different fonts, logos, and official colors. It's remarkably nitpicky, specifying that one should use *bed net* as opposed to *bednet*—it doesn't explain why the space matters so much, but apparently it does—and that one must capitalize the *But* in the organization's name. All the organization's Web pages, merchandise items, and mailings reflect this central command. You will never see a color other than black, gray, white, or their specific shade of orange on Nothing But Nets materials; nor will you ever see an unapproved font on official Nothing But Nets reports and brochures. But the brand binder goes further. It also talks about ways volunteers can help, explains the history of the organization, and gives key facts and statistics. And it even prescribes a very specific tone to be used in Nothing But Nets work: staffers are always to try to express effective solutions to an urgent need while sloughing off guilt as a means of motivating donors.

This may seem ridiculously authoritarian, especially since they're all grown-ups at Nothing But Nets. But maintaining its distinct identity is actually crucial. Matters of grammar, color, and syntax may not seem that important, but think about it: Nothing But Nets is a common phrase on any basketball court in the world. They picked a catchy name, but also one that could breed confusion, so how do you distinguish the organization? Through diligence. By splitting hairs.

Next, you have to make sure those guidelines don't migrate to their most common resting place: in the bottom drawer of the marketing and communications team members' desks. As impressively comprehensive as Nothing But Nets' brand binder may be, I wonder if they could have boiled it down to a page of essentials. I think communications guidelines should be one page long, pasted on the office or cubicle wall of every single employee. They are not just for the marketing department. Everyone should be responsible for upholding consistency and guarding the brand. The guidelines should be shared with every board member too, so that they can describe the company's brand simply, pinpoint its uniqueness, and name its relevance to a specific target market.

REVIEW YOUR BRAND POSITION REGULARLY.

Are you still the *only* or *cheaper*? Have you added new programs that shift your simple statement to something else? Has your target market changed? If you answered "I don't know" to any of those questions—if you had to think about asking someone else for the information—then you have a problem.

Every summer DoSomething.org's staff spends a full day just sitting around analyzing our stats, talking about our target market. The mantra has become *What does the data say?* Two years ago we skewed tween, hitting the twelve-to-thirteen-year-old girls. Now the data tells us that we've aged up, attracting more teenagers. How does this affect us? It tells us we need to change the programs we

offer, the language we use on the site, and even some of our policies and procedures. Brands shift as audiences change.

That communications guide should be edited every year. And your whole team should not just be briefed on it or be forced to read it; they should participate in a conversation about the brand tone, the target market, and key words to use or avoid. As suggested in Chapter 1, this exercise should include the staff at every level, in every corner of the company. Because the brand is the heart of your company. It affects everything.

CHOOSE PARTNERSHIPS ACCORDING TO YOUR BRAND GUIDELINES.

Ever since junior high, we've all known that we're often judged by the people we're associated with. (Do you spend all your time in between classes listening to heavy metal and drinking beer behind the school? Hmmm. Good luck convincing your principal and parents that you're not troubled. You might well be an angel, but if you hang with the devil, are you really pure?)

Business is no different. Your reputation doesn't exist in isolation; in fact, it's a dynamic, ever-changing creature, shaped and colored by every person and every partnership your company is associated with.

Because so much of our funding depends on our reputations, not-for-profits are especially sensitive to the alliances we form. We're even careful about the support we accept. (We're not unique in that regard: politicians these days know all about the perils of being identified with unseemly donors.) We know that one wrong move can alter, dilute, or damage a brand. An action that might offer short-term benefits (a big infusion of new money!) can have a negative long-term impact, not just on the program or on that one office, but on the entire brand.

When it comes to fund-raising, the managers of a not-for-profit brand must sometimes make tough choices in order to protect it.

Would you accept $10,000 from Osama bin Laden? Absolutely not. Would you accept $1 million from Osama bin Laden? Probably not . . . but some organizations would certainly find it a bit more tempting. Would you accept $10 million from Osama bin Laden? The answer is, "Would I have to publicize who it came from?"

That's an extreme example. But what if a tobacco company wanted to contribute to your shelter for battered women? Tobacco companies make a product that causes cancer but has no direct correlation to domestic violence. It's a gray area, right? Teach For America has an explicit no-tobacco-money policy, which makes sense for two reasons. First, the organization is focused on the well-being of children, to which the business of selling tobacco, a product not legally available to minors, seems antithetical. Second and less obvious, one of Teach For America's board members and major donors is incredibly passionate about the ills of the tobacco industry.

Truly, there's nothing like the prospect of a lucrative partnership to get you to start the litany of justification and rationalization that leads to compromise. We in the oh-so-principled not-for-profit world may not be in the business of making money, but we aren't immune to the temptations of growth. We have to reach increasingly ambitious financial targets to keep our stakeholders happy and meet the demands of our programming. Often we're tempted to take the money and run—as fast as we can, from our consciences and our brand guidelines.

The risks are often much subtler than these examples. When Dress for Success was just getting off the ground, I had a $5,000 inheritance from my Poppy Max and the idea. That was it. The very sweet nuns on my board of directors had suggested that I put the $5,000 in a CD so we could earn interest on it. I followed their advice and put the entire $5,000 in a six-month CD at the bank. The moral of this story? Never take financial advice from nuns. Holy as their counsel may have been, it meant we started the organization with no money. Then along came Sears, which wanted to partner with us and give us a $10,000 contribution—a sum twice the size of our entire asset base . . . which was untouchable, locked in that CD.

Sears proposed pairing our clients with editors from twelve major fashion publications. Together they'd rummage through the racks at Sears in search of new suits to wear to their job interviews. Basically, our clients were the bait to get the likes of *Vogue*'s André Leon Talley to experience the "softer side of Sears." In addition to the money, we'd potentially receive an enormous amount of media coverage, as each editor would write about his or her experience.

I turned down the partnership. While we would have benefited in the short term, it would have harmed our brand in the long term. We knew we were going to need a lot of suits—suits that women could wear to job interviews at Goldman Sachs and other posh venues. Once we partnered with Sears, we'd be affiliated with its image, which might scare off the high-end brands that we really wanted as partners. Dress for Success would have debuted at the lower end of the retail spectrum, connected with the Sears brand. It would have been a "category killer," meaning that once we were so publicly tied to Sears, no other major retailer would have touched us. We'd be "theirs." So we said a word rarely uttered by not-for-profits to potential funders: *no.*

Shortly thereafter, we forged very public partnerships with Coach and with Ferragamo. Every client left with a new Coach handbag—a symbol of aspiration that would build her confidence and make her proud. And many clients left wearing comfortable, sturdy, fashionable new Ferragamo shoes that made them smile, walk just a little taller, and hold their chins just a little higher.

The happy story doesn't end there. Sears ended up using their partnership idea with another organization, which wasn't the right fit for a plan that had really been designed for us. They made no more than a tiny blip on the publicity radar. The next year Sears called us again. This time they proposed giving us $150,000 (!) and $50,000 worth of plus-size suits and blouses. We needed these items badly, as our average client's size was 18. By this point, we had already established a reputation for providing quality apparel and shoes to help our clients land jobs. We knew our potential partners saw us as classy, professional, and stylish—a brand they'd feel

comfortable linking up with. And working women—our individual donors—felt they could trust us to redistribute their sometimes sentimentally valuable, often pricey, gently worn suits.

So we did the campaign with Sears. It was a huge success. I will never forget the image of André Leon Talley, a giant not just in his sector but also in person, sashaying to the accessories department. He then plowed through dozens of pleather handbags, in search of one to build an outfit around. (His strategy, not mine.)

The lesson is, don't be afraid to say no. Your brand is precious, and preserving it can take a gargantuan effort—and huge amounts of willpower. Pick your partners carefully, assess the timing of a potential pairing, and look at the alliance's broad implications, not just for your market but for other, future partnerships as well.

ELEVEN QUESTIONS TO GET YOU STARTED:
Do More with Your Brand

Some of the most valuable and recognizable brands in the world are those of not-for-profit companies. Often, they're not huge operations, especially when measured against your typical corporation. Wikipedia, for instance, has an annual budget of approximately $5 million—that's an *m*, not a *b*. But you don't necessarily need many millions to build a strong brand. You don't need the Super Bowl ad. You don't need consultants to add an exclamation point to your name, design a new letterhead, or concoct a new logo. You don't need to throw money at an outside agency (or more likely, a team of them) to come up with a tagline, a campaign, or a brand strategy. (One idea is to create an internal competition for the employees you're already paying, who know you best, and ask them to dream up a few.)

You could do all those things, but that wouldn't necessarily

make your brand any stronger, better, or more authentic to consumers. What makes a strong brand? Creativity, hard work, soul, and smart strategies like the ones I've outlined in this chapter. Try asking these questions. They won't cost you a dime.

1. If your brand were a car, what kind of car would it be? What color? Old, used, new? What price point? Would everyone in your company have a similar answer?

2. Can you describe your brand as the *first*, the *only*, *faster*, *better*, or *cheaper*? If not, you're toast.

3. Who is your brand relevant to? Describe him or her in as much detail as possible. How old is he? How does she spend her day? Her nights? Weekends?

4. Ask your office manager, your receptionist, and your cafeteria serving staff to describe your company in one sentence. Those people are your frontline soldiers who hear and see every department, at every level. Really listen to how they answer the question.

5. When was the last time members of various work teams, at diverse levels of the company, spent more than two hours together just looking at data and talking about the brand—without a specific brainstorm topic on the table?

6. Who are your five most visible partners? What do you think your target market thinks of them?

7. Do you have standards for selecting partners? Are they based on multiple elements or just on price? Size? Convenience?

8. How does your mom or husband or child describe the company where you work? Is it a more simple and accurate description than the one you've been instructed to recite?

9. Do you have written brand guidelines for your company? A booklet? A one-page memo? An e-mail that was sent "to all" last year? Who wrote it? How was it put together?

10. Are there words that are *nevers* for your brand? (For example, in soccer you never use your hands unless you are the goalie.) Do you have banned words? Should you?

11. What does the data say? When was the last time you asked yourself this question?

3

DO MORE WITH YOUR EXTERNAL PEOPLE

CORPORATIONS OFTEN PAY THEIR brand ambassadors thousands of dollars, and if that person has a recognizable face and a career in the movies, the bill could run into the millions. Athletes are thrown money to wear logos on their sleeves. In good times the armies of salespeople pile up the commissions. But even a small, relatively underfunded not-for-profit can easily have a sales force of millions. And it usually doesn't cost a penny.

To understand how it works, all you have to do is to walk into a gym anywhere in America (or a gym in Dubai full of American-educated businessmen) at peak times. I guarantee you'll see the same thing: the weights, the water cooler, the towels, the mirrors, the treadmills—and lots and lots of sweaty college T-shirts. Our universities have pulled off one of the cleverest tricks in branding: somehow, they've churned out legions of lifelong ambassadors. Not only have they avoided putting these folks on their payroll; in most cases, those sweaty guys actually *paid for* the honor of wearing that

brand, sometimes to the tune of thousands of dollars in tuition, fees, and T-shirt costs.

To be fair, colleges and universities invest heavily in cultivating their ambassadorial corps. They send out alumni magazines. They create alumni clubs. They host alumni events. They organize online alumni groups. Parents of current students are invited to the school one weekend each year. Beyond the alumni, community-relations offices work hard to develop relationships with townies. Local retailers, politicians, residents, and media aren't going to give and promote as alumni might, but it serves a school well not to have the locals as opposition. Then there are the many others who have some tie to the college, from contractors and suppliers, to the extended families and friends of proud alumni, to some guy who picked up branded lacrosse shorts long ago on a random campus visit. All the people in these concentric circles of a university community could potentially be seen with that COLLEGE emblazoned across their chests at the gym on a Saturday morning, in the front yard mowing the lawn, or at the grocery store buying eggs. And this is how not-for-profits think of our "external people": every one of them is a potential ambassador. Exactly how do we get people not on our payroll to sell our brand? Here are some of our best-kept secrets for getting more from our unpaid ambassadors.

CONSIDER EVERYONE A POTENTIAL AMBASSADOR.

The first step to unleashing your army of ambassadors is to realize how big your militia potentially could be. The core is the group of believers that every company has. Beyond employees, the core includes individuals who are financially or emotionally invested in the company's prosperity: your suppliers, customers, partners, and stockholders; community groups that depend on your firm's charitable donations; and nearly anyone else who comes in contact with your company's products, services, or brand. Even the ex-girlfriend of your mail clerk is part of this core group.

Without any effort on your part, your company's good name is already out there in ways you may not realize. Think of your former employees. The fact that they once worked for your bank is proudly displayed on their résumé and their LinkedIn profile for all to see. And did you know that the janitorial service that you hired used the fact that you are a client to secure other clients in your neighborhood? And how about that trusty old mail carrier, who's been delivering your bills every day for years, despite downpours, golf-ball-size hail, and *Lawrence of Arabia* heat? Do you think of these people as part of your team? They're thinking of you, every day.

Your challenge, should you choose to accept it, is to maximize the possible positive effects of the yea-sayers and to minimize the repercussions of the nay-sayers. I recommend that you accept the challenge, because they're thinking about you and talking about you whether you like it or not. Some may be bitter, like the hypothetical former employee of Coca-Cola; the day he left the company, he switched to Pepsi and reportedly never let a sip of Coke pass his lips again. On the other end of the spectrum, you have my husband's grandfather, a longtime JCPenney employee who, until the day he died, still faithfully read the monthly employee newsletter, kept in touch with friends from back in the day, and popped into the store whenever he could. Will your former employees be like the disgruntled Coke alum or Grandpa Dean? That depends more on you than on them.

Traditionally, in the corporate sector, only salespeople and their superiors make direct pitches, and only a select few are ever tapped to make formal presentations to customers. In not-for-profits, though, we don't limit our selling to the fund-raising staff. Everyone connected to the organization—especially these external people—is potential sales staff. We hope that everyone sells, whether it's the intern who's just here for the summer or the business mogul on our board of directors. Truly, they are all ambassadors, representatives of our brand in external markets. We need every one we can get.

Advocacy can take many forms. Advocacy may be a summer volunteer from years ago who is now using his significant contacts

to generate donations to achieve a particular goal. Advocacy may be the techie son of an office manager donating his geeked-out brain to help the not-for-profit build a better website. Advocacy may even be the friend of a friend whom I invited on the spur of the moment to a fund-raising event, where he loved the DJ so much that he tweeted about how cool the party was, sending good vibes about my organization to all 400 of his Twitter followers and 750 Facebook friends. Cost? Zilch.

If you're selling toothpaste or tractors or maybe a B2B software product, you may not think your external people will help you with your sales and your reputation as much as I claim. You would be wrong. You'd be surprised how many people believe in your brand, and how many potential evangelists you have out there. They can do a lot for your company if you provide them with the motivation—and means—to help you.

TREAT YOUR EXTERNAL PEOPLE AS YOU'D LIKE THEM TO TREAT YOU.

The first step to energizing ambassadors is to show that you care about them. Kindness and thoughtfulness are not only good policies for life, they're effective means of winning people over. When people feel consistently respected and cared for, they become more than the sum of their roles and responsibilities; you develop a relationship. They become stakeholders, fans, and friends.

Charles Best, the founder of DonorsChoose.org, is adamant about expressing kindness and active gratitude to those who contribute to his cause. The DonorsChoose.org website presents individual requests from teachers in underfunded public schools. Featured projects have a specific ask, and donors can search the website for projects that resonate with them; one teacher requested donations of books including the *Goosebumps* series by R. L. Stine, which he thought would resonate with the young readers—and especially the nonreaders—in his class, while another wanted funding to take

kids to visit a prestigious college two hours away, where they could get a glimpse of what could be if they applied themselves diligently. A donor then selects a project and contributes to its completion.

Charles and his staff do not let these donors slip away into cyberspace—they are skilled at showing gratitude and staying in touch. He sends cameras along with the donations, requiring teachers to take pictures of the projects that the donors enabled. Charles then collects those pictures and sends them back to the donor, accompanied by thank-you notes from the children. The dividends of this strategy are clear, Charles says. One woman so appreciated those photos that she pasted them on the back of her door so that every time she left her home, she would see them. Her late husband had actually been the donor. Still overwhelmed by grief, she said that seeing what a nice thing he had done while he was alive—and knowing that his actions were appreciated—was a great source of comfort.

I know I'm starting to sound a little like Miss Manners, but the best organizations display thoughtfulness and graciousness from top to bottom. A simple litmus test of kindness is how people at any given company answer their phones. First, is there even a real person answering the phone? I realize that from a short-term economic standpoint, automated responses sometimes make sense. But even the most polite, efficient automated system in the world is never going to come across as kind or, well, personal. Having a live human being answer the phone is a small way to show that you care about the people who are calling your office.

I don't care if it's the CEO, the customer service representative, or the receptionist: when an organization treats its callers in a consistently friendly, helpful manner, it usually displays that attitude to all stakeholders. When you call a Girl Scouts office anywhere in the world, someone always answers the phone by saying, "Hello, Girl Scouts, where girls grow strong!" It's more than the words that are powerful—it's the positive attitude behind them. Sure, sometimes people have grumpy days and those words sound garbled or forced, but the intention is there. That the leadership has taken the time

to consider how callers are greeted suggests thoughtfulness. The greeting on the phone—that ever-important first impression—is intended to rope you into the fold immediately.

While I was conducting interviews for this book, I knew that at any time, day or night, I could reach out to John Lilly, CEO of Mozilla. Every time I promised that I was posing one last follow-up question, Lilly reassured me that he was happy to help however possible. Speaking on the phone and being expeditiously responsive, he demonstrated that he is nothing short of caring and compassionate. He runs one of the biggest Internet companies in the world, yet he always had time to share his thoughts. It is this kind of responsiveness that retains interest and creates stakeholders. Before my interactions with Lilly, I casually vacillated between using as my browser Mozilla Firefox and Internet Explorer, but now I'm a dedicated Mozilla girl—in fact, I'm an evangelical missionary for the brand. (Do you use it yet? You should.) His kindness converted me.

The speed and manner in which your company responds to calls reflect how much you value and respect the person who is making them, and in our business we can't afford to underestimate anyone's value. Idealist.org is the open-source website for not-for-profit jobs and volunteer opportunities around the world. Despite the global market and the challenges of time zones, the organization has set up a system that ensures that staff members respond promptly to queries. Each day the e-mails and phone calls are split among the various employees according to their expertise, which means no one person is "stuck" doing customer service. It is then everyone's job to respond before the day's end, ensuring that no request is left unanswered for more than twenty-four hours.

SEEK FEEDBACK FROM EVERYONE, NOT JUST CUSTOMERS.

You don't have to care about external people just for the sake of caring: there's a point to it for your business. They can offer you things,

and an important one is feedback. It's normal to seek feedback from your customers, but do you seek it from your vendors? From former employees? From the public? And if you do collect feedback, is it by having people fill out little forms that pile up and collect dust in the human resources department, or do you integrate their feedback into your internal decision-making?

Let me be clear about what I mean by feedback. We've all ignored a gazillion comment cards and annoying questionnaires. Good feedback—well-designed studies and smartly conceived surveys—can and should be more than a series of answers to bubble-in questions, rating various things on scales of one to ten or *poor* to *excellent* or *strongly disagree* to *strongly agree*. In a few exemplary instances, feedback rises to an entirely new level altogether. It can even help your company do its own work.

DonorsChoose has an unusual decision-making strategy that's based, to a surprising degree, on external feedback. Each of the teacher requests in the DonorsChoose online marketplace has to be vetted before the giving public can see it. At one point the organization considered hiring staffers exclusively to handle the time-consuming task of validating those teacher requests. But the DonorsChoose leadership thought there must be another way, another more effective and more efficient way. Surely, they thought, there must be a tech-assisted solution.

Taking a cue from Wikipedia, they have their users—the teachers—vet each other's project requests. Who could give better feedback than the people who use the system on a regular basis? "We are taking a core part of our business—the pillar of our operation—and we've turned it over to our user base," says CEO Charles Best. "Of course, it's the same as the Tom Sawyer method to convince his friends that whitewashing the fence is a privilege. You are doing more than turning your customers into advocates. You are turning your advocates into staff."

MAKE IT EASY FOR OUTSIDERS TO BE INSIDERS.

People are busy. People are stressed. People have a lot of different things going on. People are already multitasking too much. Even if you're nice to people on the phone and even if you think you have a way to turn your advocates into de facto staff, how do you convince them to participate? How do you convert them to your cause? How do you make it easy—irresistible, even—to help?

The brand can do a lot for you. It's difficult to believe in an ill-defined or vague organizational message. It's hard to convince someone to back an uninspiring brand. And it's impossible to expect someone to sell that brand who isn't paid. Especially for those of us in the not-for-profit world, all communication must reinforce a well-defined, singularly focused message. That allows people to have a clear vision of what the organization is trying to accomplish and what it values. The simplicity and power of the message encourages belief. It also enables believers to communicate their creed to others. It is impossible to convince a friend to try a product or visit a website or donate money if in the same breath you are unable to explain, concisely and memorably, why they should bother and why they ought to care.

Share Our Strength is the not-for-profit that battles the problem, all too invisible to most of us, of child hunger in America. Kids all across this country aren't getting enough to eat, and malnutrition has an incredible knock-on effect on their education and their futures. Many of us have no idea that this is happening in the richest country in the world. So when dynamo Billy Shore, the founder and CEO of Share Our Strength, talks about this problem, people are almost always moved to help. The brand and its message, simple and clear, resonate. But how does Share Our Strength help? What does it do?

The genius of Share Our Strength is that it has made answering those questions so easy. It has a slew of well-designed programs that are easily accessible to people across the nation. By "easily accessible," I mean that they cleverly integrate help for the organization

into activities that both reinforce the message and barely require you to alter your routine. It's difficult *not* to help. For instance, the Great American Dine Out is a week in which supporters of Share Our Strength are encouraged to go out to eat in restaurants that have pledged a portion of their proceeds to the charity. I mean, people gotta eat, right?

If a ginormous corporation were launching a for-profit analog to that campaign, I'd imagine it would involve a hearty media spend—full-page advertisements in newspapers and maybe a few glossy national magazines; billboards in key locations; and perhaps even some radio and TV spots for the truly flush. Share Our Strength doesn't typically have the budget to afford that kind of promotion. And even if it did, the organization doesn't necessarily want to do that kind of advertising, because the demands on the creative are incredibly high. In a relatively small layout space, which shouldn't be particularly text-heavy, you have to explain to the market what your product is first. Then you have to convince them to participate.

But what if you've already put to diligent work some of the ideas from earlier in this chapter? What if you've started to think about those brand ambassadors-in-waiting? Share Our Strength has a large database that comprises the names and contact info of anyone who has ever come in contact with the organization. These are the folks to whom it vigorously promotes the Great American Dine Out. And the organization gets a great return ($500,000 in its first year) on its relatively minimal investment.

NEVER BREAK UP WITH YOUR AMBASSADORS. EVER.

The way Share Our Strength taps into its networks makes me think of a summer I once spent working in a Nantucket deli, slicing meat. Well, actually, I lasted only four weeks, but those four long weeks have stayed with me. I received only two paychecks and had not worked there long enough to qualify for union membership, but that work experience was on my résumé until I graduated from col-

lege. Now, twenty years later, every time I walk into a grocery store or stroll past a Subway or see someone bite into a grinder, I think about that deli and some of the less-than-hygienic practices I witnessed there. My stomach still churns a little bit as I remember. I will reflexively turn to the person I am with—or a stranger standing next to me—and mention that I once worked in a deli and still don't eat ham. Over the years I suspect that I have turned a lot of people off eating ham—and from having lunch with me.

I have not been back to that deli in twenty years. Heck, I haven't even been back to Nantucket. And yet I still think of myself as a former member of that team. I have an intimate knowledge of the place. I once wore a hairnet for four whole weeks because of it! That deli is in me forever. I guess I'd join an alumni association if someone ever started one.

Some smart not-for-profits have grown wise to this phenomenon of people's elephant-like memory of their past jobs and are especially willing to exploit it when the alums think good thoughts. Teach For America is a premier example of an organization that assiduously cultivates—even coddles—its alumni. TFA actually has an office of alumni relations headed by a full-time director. The office organizes reunions, conferences, and summits and even publishes an alumni magazine. It seeks partnerships with graduate schools to help alumni afford postgraduate education. On the TFA website "alumni services" is a prominent tab, and on its automated phone menu it's one of the first options.

By offering them such an extensive range of real programs, Teach For America has developed a close—and certainly long-term— relationship with its alumni. It's a brilliant tactic—and good business. These people have already demonstrated extreme interest in and dedication to the organization. They have not stopped caring about these issues just because they no longer work for Teach For America. They might even soon have salaries that will enable them to further the organization's mission in a significant way.

Over the years Teach For America's alumni have become one of its most powerful assets. Many are now in positions of great

influence. Michelle Rhee, an early TFA teacher who worked in an inner-city Baltimore school, founded the not-for-profit New Teacher Project, and now heads a troubled Washington, D.C., school district; she is trying to apply some of what she learned in her not-for-profit career to the public sector. Andy Moffet, an early TFA teacher in Houston, is now a McKinsey consultant to a little shop called the Bill & Melinda Gates Foundation, on their education grant-making. Other TFA alumni are school board members, education policy-makers, and lawyers. So many alumni have run for public office that TFA created a full-time position and an institute to train these people for political life. Countless others are in significant corporate jobs—and in equally significant informal employment as unpaid recruiter-donor-advocates. TFA's "external people" have had an effect on the organization that is nothing short of massive. Why? In part because TFA's philosophy is to hold on to these people. With apologies to the Eagles band, I suppose Teach For America is like the Hotel California: you can check in but you can never leave.

Less formal but just as impressive is the Human Rights Campaign's intern alumni program. It's a simple listserv—but to that list are sent job postings, invitations to events, requests for volunteers, and media alerts. Those former interns have become like an HRC militia, ready to leap for their former employer at any moment, even years later.

Both Goldman Sachs and McKinsey & Company do a notable job of remaining in contact with former employees. In fact, these shops have developed a reputation as finishing schools for businesspeople. Spending two years at one of these firms is a springboard to future success. And Goldman and McKinsey know it. They expect their employees to leave for other pastures and to reflect fondly on their career beginnings there. Not surprisingly, those former employees later send a heck of a lot of business back to Goldman and to McKinsey. Several newspapers and magazines have recently written about this phenomenon, almost suggesting there exists a nefarious plot for Goldman to rule to world. But maybe it's just smart business.

The flip side is that some companies turn the exit process into an exile process. They berate people for leaving, profess not to understand how they could do such a thing—even if it's clearly for a better, higher-paying job—and insist that they are making a mistake that they will come to regret. Noncompete agreements warn of possible legal action if they do X or Y, and other general unpleasantness abounds. And all too often we've seen on the news burly security guards unceremoniously escorting unfortunate ex-employees to the front door.

Whenever I see those pictures or hear these stories, I always have to wonder why. Why would any company want people to walk out its door with the raw materials for lifelong resentment and long-term bitterness toward the firm and its brand? Why would a company want its former employees' last memory of the place to be public humiliation?

No doubt some managers feel betrayed when a valued employee leaves. Too bad—this isn't about you, Mr. Manager. Get over your hurt self. It's not good for any organization to be sending discontented ex-employees out into the wider world. Try to see the situation from the worker's point of view. Career coaches always advise exiting employees not to burn bridges. Why should it be any different from the other end of the bridge?

I guess it's natural for most corporations to forget about former employees—out of utility, out of sight, out of mind. But over time it's a mistake: people will leave and move on, but they'll always have their memories. They'll always be former employees. The odds are that most of them had good experiences at the company—and some had great experiences. Those in this good-to-great group are potentially terrific promoters of the brand, but most companies don't give these individuals the chance to promote. Instead, it's "out of site, out of mind"—they just ignore that entire category of talent.

It's hard for me to overemphasize that this is a huge, stupid mistake. Not-for-profits have learned how useful alumni are, both directly and indirectly, at selling the brand. They can sell a prospective employee on joining the company; they can contribute their

expertise to help the company put together a customer pitch. This is an important lesson for for-profits too.

Let's go back to the university model I mentioned earlier. Just about every college and university puts an emphasis on alumni relations, because they know that in the coming decades these people will be their biggest supporters—not just in sports but also and especially in terms of financial donations. Why should it be any different for a big business?

I think that corporations should create the job of alumni-relations director. This person would conjure ways to cultivate the many ex-employees out in the marketplace working as great advocates. Develop a section of the corporate website targeting alumni. Establish an open forum so that they can reminisce and reconnect with other ex-employees. Bring people together for face-to-face reunions. Get them to contribute some of their institutional memories. Send them coupons. Remind them of their connections with holiday cards. Tell them how the company's doing.

All this makes former employees feel valued and included. It turns them from neglected former stakeholders into active advocates. If they're going to sell the company, they need to feel like they still belong.

REMEMBER THAT WORD OF MOUTH IS THE SINGLE BEST FORM OF MARKETING.

This chapter is sort of about finding fans who aren't on your payroll, but it's really about cultivating evangelists. There's a significant difference between a fan and an evangelist. A fan really, really likes something, but an evangelist really, really likes something so much that he or she can't help but tell others. They think the something is so good that they just have to let everyone else know. If you wanted to, you could also call them marketers.

In the not-for-profit world, we appreciate our fans. We like it when they give us $50 donations just before Christmas, and we ap-

preciate when they leave us small bequests when they die. But we love our evangelists, because they're the ones who will send us a check *and* tweet all their friends about us *and* encourage a high-school service organization to hold a bake sale for us *and* organize a screening at church of a tearjerker documentary that's sure to get all the like-minded folks in their circle to care and maybe even give to the good cause.

Not-for-profits have developed different strategies for helping potential evangelists spread the word, and there are some lessons here for the for-profit world. The first is, don't be afraid of the various venues in which people interact these days. The tech-savvier among you already know the power of technology to bring people together and to build new settings in which they interact. But without the Internet, we wouldn't have trailblazers like Eric Ding.

Born in China, Eric and his family immigrated to the United States when he was five. As a teenager, Eric developed a baseball-size malignant tumor in his chest. When cancer was diagnosed, the number five turned out to have great significance for him: his doctors told him he had five years left to live.

Unfortunately for the cancer, Eric had other plans. By his senior year he had recovered sufficiently to earn varsity letters in track and cross-country. Today, cancer-free, he is known as the creator of a pioneering Facebook group that suggested the potential of social networking for not-for-profit marketing. Within six months of its creation, the Campaign for Cancer Prevention had more than 2.2 million supporters—and it has now surpassed the 3 million mark.

The beauty of Eric's creation is that it tapped the networks of a few people he knew, then those of hundreds and thousands and millions of people he didn't know. When Facebook friends saw other Facebook friends joining this group, they wondered why, clicked on the link, and then often joined themselves. He made it so easy—just click.

Monetizing those clicks and turning those group members into active supporters, of course, is a much bigger challenge. But Ding's

story illustrates that when you go where the people are, get your story into their circles, and then make it easy for them to act on their excitement, they will.

At DoSomething.org our studies show us that kids are four times more likely to actively volunteer if a friend asks them to. So we make it easy. The number one way that teens communicate is via text messaging. If you text "DoSomething" to 30644, we'll send you a volunteer opportunity in your zip code, twice a month. You can forward it to friends, right from the palm of your hand. We've enabled teens to do our marketing for us, via a mechanism they use all day (and night?) long. To date, sixty thousand kids are signed up for the service, with a whopping 30 percent actually using it to find and participate in a volunteer activity.

ALIGN INCENTIVES.

By now, you may be wondering why these external people I keep extolling should be so happy to act as salespeople. Why should they bother to help?

One obvious lure is stuff. You probably have some incentives you can offer them at relatively low cost. For instance, a few times a year DoSomething.org organizes huge, star-studded fun events. The ticket price is anywhere from $250 to $5,000 a head, far beyond most student budgets. But we always offer our former interns free tickets. After all, those kids gave us a summer of their lives for free. They are smart, ambitious people who know us well. Someday some of them might want to come back and work for us. Many more (I hope) will be quite rich and will want to give us piles of their money. So why not include them? It's a great investment.

Any retailer would be wise to embrace this principle by, say, offering all employees 5 percent discounts for life. It would create loyal customers and have a ripple effect with their friends and fami-lies, who will no doubt try to exploit that discount as well. Such tokens of appreciation are simply good business because they gener-

ate continued patronage as well as good feelings and could even be an incentive for new hires. Home Depot employees who leave the company are still going to be performing do-it-yourself projects in their own homes and gardens. Doesn't Home Depot want them to keep shopping in its stores, long after they stop working there? Give them a discount for life. The sales will come back in spades.

USE STAKEHOLDERS AS TALENT HEADHUNTERS.

Three years ago DoSomething.org hired a public relations firm. Someone at that firm had e-mailed and phoned me repeatedly for a few months trying to get our business. It occurred to me that his persistence was exactly the trait I wanted in a PR firm. So we hired his agency, agreeing to a monthly retainer for a year. Within the first three months that diligent employee left, and so had four other people—out of a firm of maybe fifteen full-time employees. The last time I saw so many people leave so quickly was while in a movie theater watching Kevin Costner's *Waterworld*.

Eventually we escaped our contract and found a great new—and stable—PR firm. But I kept in contact with some of those escapees from the original firm, who all landed at other agencies. When we have job positions available, I circulate those descriptions pretty widely—even to these people. And they always send me fantastic leads. Why? Because having been on our account, they know our business. Because my humane treatment of them leads them to believe that I would be a humane person to work for. And because they know there's only upside in currying goodwill with me. Someday, after all, I might be a client again.

Many companies artificially limit their referral networks, figuring that their real opportunities will come from a small but select circle of quality individuals and groups. But not-for-profits have learned that some of their best opportunities come from unexpected and unlikely places. A huge donor might come through your brother-in-law's cousin, whom you met at a party. A former volunteer might

help turn his employer into a valuable corporate sponsor. The guy who builds your trade show booth might build a booth for another company and discover that it's in need of the services your company provides. An ex-employee might join a company that requires the service your company provides. A former board member might join another corporate board and realize that the two companies would be ideal partners in a joint venture.

Every company recognizes the importance of referral sources, but not everyone recognizes how widely one should really trawl for these sources. Finding the right people and convincing them to join is the crux of recruitment. Searches sometimes go global, requiring contacts in out-of-the-way places. In addition, many jobs have become highly specialized, demanding expertise in a narrow area to make the right hiring decision. Your external partners could be in a good position to convince a high performer to join your firm, but will that outsider make the introduction? The answer depends on you.

OUTSIDE BELIEVERS CAN BE A GREAT SOURCE OF INNOVATION.

Outsiders aren't just good sources for referrals—sometimes they're great sources of creative ideas that can help us do our work better or even transform our operations. People who work for not-for-profits tend to be entrepreneurial and open to great ideas, no matter where they come from. Most are pretty young, too, and relatively unburdened by the not-invented-here syndrome.

Some not-for-profits' best fund-raising campaigns and alliances have originated outside their offices. A donor might call up with an idea, or a former intern might offer an unexpectedly terrific suggestion. One summer at DoSomething.org we had a high-school intern named Heather. She was smart, quick, and organized. A good kid. We were sad to see her head back to school that fall. A couple of months into the semester, she phoned me with an idea.

Now a senior in high school, she was the president of her school's community service club, which in her words "was totally lame." The club had to pay national dues, follow a prescribed "community service" plan, and fax in the results. "This is so last century," she said. "I mean, if we wanna change something, we just throw up a Facebook group and make it happen. DoSomething.org ought to just make it possible for kids to create Do Something Clubs at their schools by signing up online." It was a terrific idea from the fast-talking, gum-smacking mouth of a seventeen-year-old. Now, three years later, that program exists in more than one thousand schools nationwide.

ELEVEN QUESTIONS TO GET YOU STARTED:
Do More with Your External People

Your in-house team is no doubt valuable for your success, but your external army can be just as crucial. In this chapter, I've outlined some of the places where you can look for these people and how to cultivate them. It's obviously a long-term and multifaceted process, but I believe it will produce incredible and exponentially powerful results.

The more skeptical among you may be questioning the possibility of creating believers outside your ranks. That's fine. Let the idea settle in a little bit. We in the not-for-profit world certainly have—and we're more than comfortable with it. In fact, it's largely responsible for our success. We've realized that building a corps of brand evangelists isn't an accidental by-product of our business—it has to be a conscious effort. We strive to enlist the heart, mind, and soul of every person we meet.

The methods that not-for-profits use to engage stakeholders would translate well to for-profit environments. In some ways,

they'd work even better, since many for-profits are bigger and the ripple effects would be even more powerful. But before you begin to work out the details, make sure you've embraced this one fact: *Functionaries function, believers commit.*

Corporations should recognize that believers can drive sales, produce new partnerships, generate enormous buzz, bring in new business, and reduce costs. Every person your company has ever encountered and will encounter has the capacity to become a great asset to you for years to come.

Oh, ginormous company, are you ready to listen to them? Ask yourself these questions:

1. Can you make a list of the people and partners with whom you have had only one touch? That is, people who have encountered your brand, product, or service only one time, with no further contact.

2. What negative ambassadors do you have out there? Do you have vendors or partners or former employees who don't like you? Have you reached out to them? Or, are you hoping that if you close your eyes, they will magically disappear?

3. Does your company have a LinkedIn group? Who monitors it? Does someone from your company verify that all the users have, in fact, worked there?

4. Have you ever called random people at your company to hear them answer the phone? Your customer service department? Your own assistant? Your various store managers?

5. What happens when an internship ends at your company? Assuming you don't hire that kid, do you ever see him or her again? Is there any formal relationship that remains?

6. Who handles customer service for your brand? (Notice I said *brand* and not *company*, *product*, or *service*. From Chapter 2, we know that the brand is bigger than those elements. And some of the questions coming to your help line are brand-centric, not "How do I replace the battery?" or "Is my flight on time?")

7. What is the exit process for people who leave voluntarily from your company? Do you keep in contact with them? Do they retain any benefits as a result of having worked for the company?

8. Do you reward external people for referring business to your company? Is this a formal process or an ad hoc thing?

9. When you look for feedback or post available jobs, do you think to ask these external stakeholders?

10. If you bumped into one of your customers on the street, and he said, "Hey, I love your product. Can I help you guys out?" how would you answer him? (Hint: "Buy more product" is the wrong answer.)

11. Does your company have a newsletter? Who receives it?

4

DO MORE BY ASKING SMART

SO THERE I WAS, sitting quietly in that lovely corporate conference room, nibbling on my over-engineered cookie, as those around me panicked about their lack of money to build a media component for our joint campaign. They blathered about grabbing money from some budget and going to visit so-and-so in global markets about getting some scraps from them. At one point, a senior marketing person interrupted the chitchat and announced through clenched teeth, "This is ridiculous. Can't we just tell Yahoo to do it for us?"

I wasn't sure if her question was rhetorical or was meant for someone specific in the room or on the phone. Or maybe she had some kind of telepathic hotline to the leadership of Yahoo, and they'd be sending her a response any second now by ESP or the twitch of an elbow. On reflection, it didn't sound like a question at all. It seemed more like a directive, which I thought was weird, since nobody in the room worked for Yahoo. This ginormous company didn't own Yahoo, and as far as I could tell, it had nothing to

do with Yahoo . . . except that it buys a lot of advertising space on Yahoo each year.

When a not-for-profit needs or wants money, we ask for it. Nicely. And we're actually quite good at doing it. In 2008 contributions to not-for-profits topped $300 billion. Those are donations. The people and companies and foundations who provided it were convinced to give their money away. Frankly, I've always thought it sort of shocking how much money is raised for charitable endeavors. Truly, donors' odds are worse than any game in Vegas, where you've got at least the slim chance of a return. Aside from our heartfelt thanks, a prime seat in heaven, and maybe a tax write-off, what do they get? Most of the time they don't even get their names on a building (though they usually get a mention in the annual report and a nice tote bag).

Not-for-profit leaders are amazing salespeople. You've heard the clichés about selling ice to Eskimos and swimsuits to Siberians. Well, at least you can touch ice and wear swimsuits. What we have to offer is some notion of goodness, the essence of doing something important, and a reputation for trying to change the world.

We also work in incredibly crowded space. Invariably, other not-for-profits exist in our category, competing for the same pool of donor money. All we can do is ask them to donate based on our brand, on who we are, on what we do, and on how successful we are at doing it.

Playing this sales game requires a sophisticated form of asking that would be especially relevant to for-profits at a time of so much commoditization and such a high level of competition. Can ginormous companies simply bark orders at people and actually get them to provide real value? (Would that forceful call to Yahoo really be effective?)

I started thinking about all the things we in the not-for-profit world do to essentially pick people's pockets, in the name of good.

Zainab Salbi has a gift for asking people to help her organization, Women for Women International. Her very compelling personal story often helps her make that ask. Zainab's father was

Saddam Hussein's personal pilot, and she spent many weekends around the notorious dictator. She witnessed the brutality of power, firsthand. "I would wake up with the sound of a missile hitting a neighbor's house and say, 'Okay, it's not me today.' And you go back to sleep." When Iraq invaded Kuwait, she was at school in the United States, far away from her family. She had to witness them and their friends and neighbors go through intense strife—through the telephone and letters and other snippets of information that made their way to her overseas. It was unbearable. "So I know about war. I know about living in war and about survival. And I also know about wanting to help when you're miles away." She saw the suffering in her home country, people she knew. Her own experiences of the Iran-Iraq war inspired her to care for the "backline" victims of war, the women and children who are affected.

In 1993 Salbi started Women for Women International, which has since helped more than 268,000 women and distributed more than $78 million in direct aid and microcredit loans. While the organization hosts gala events and writes applications to foundations, it's the $11 million that she raises annually from online contributions that I find particularly astounding. She acquires these gifts without spending any face time with the donors, without showing them her pleading brown eyes or letting them hear her accent, which always reminds me of her personal journey. She is able to convince people to give her $11 million over the Internet.

Some people give away their bank account numbers to those poor Nigerians who have won the lottery and just can't seem to access their bank account so they'd like to borrow mine in exchange for 10 percent of the winnings. That scam I understand—there is a chance of financial return. But how amazing is the e-mail that coaxes $11 million out of people's pockets without the promise of any return? How do you raise money when what you offer in return is zilch?

It helps that Salbi's cause is compelling. Her organization is one of the few on the ground in several of the countries where it operates. It helps enormous numbers of women, by giving them

not just aid but a hand in developing a trade and starting a business. Women for Women International is awesome. But to be able to convey all of this to a stranger, and by e-mail? There is magic there, and alchemy.

Don't you want some of that magic dust? You spend a lot of time selling too—to potential employees, to internal team members (telling them to do more or to do things differently), to customers, to suppliers, to vendors. You ask all day long. Do you do it well? Do you do it Salbi-style? Could you procure $11 million in support per year without any face time?

Here are some tips from the not-for-profit world, on asking for (and getting) what you need.

FIND THE SHARED INTERESTS.

We have two ears and one mouth for a reason—we should listen 66 percent of the time. (At least!) In business the best type of listening is sitting one-on-one with a prospect and getting to know his history, interests, quirks, worries, joys, annoyances, and likes. When I'm pitching a potential donor, I have three questions in mind:

- Why does this person care about what we're doing?

- What does he need from us?

- How can we best meet his specific requirements?

You'll notice that these questions put the prospect first and us second. That's how you have to frame your pitch—sure, it's about you getting something you need, but the decision is theirs. The thing you need is theirs. Consequently, the focus is on them.

Peter Wilderotter has been raising money for not-for-profits for nearly forty years. He has had extensive fund-raising experiences in a host of issue areas, from civil rights to women's rights to public radio. Today he focuses on spinal injury, as the CEO of the Christo-

pher and Dana Reeve Foundation, which was created following the tragic paralyzation of actor Christopher Reeve (*Superman*). Over the course of his career Peter has personally raised some $500 million for charity. And yet he rarely asks people for money. Perhaps one percent of his time is spent making an actual pitch. Instead, he says, "I talk about the mission and am interested in learning about you and what interests you."

Peter has found that if he is talking to the right person—the individual with a particular interest in the area of his not-for-profit—and if he presents his case well, they will naturally respond. If, for instance, he meets someone whose sibling has a spinal cord injury, she will want to get involved if Peter explains the strides their funded research is making in improving muscle regeneration and extending life expectancy.

It may seem hard to raise money in what is apparently a narrow field. After all, how many people are truly passionate about improving the quality of life for those suffering from spinal injury? When the served population is relatively small, and when the solution lies in research that could take decades, it is difficult to lure donors. But Peter notes that the intersection between a cause and potential donors' interests is bigger than most people assume. Even if you meet someone who doesn't have a close friend or relative with a spinal cord injury, the odds are that this person knows of someone with such an injury or has been moved by a story about a spinal cord injury, such as Christopher Reeve's well-known tale.

Think about where your organization's purpose intersects with a potential customer's area of interest—or if that customer is totally a wrong fit. It won't take long. Once you do find the intersection, you can focus attention on it, make clear that it is a mutual area of interest, and have a springboard for a concrete discussion.

DON'T CONFUSE BUSINESS AND FRIENDSHIP.

Given that I've just suggested that you get to know your sales targets well, it might seem contradictory to now say that you shouldn't become their friends. Don't not-for-profits try to form friendships with donors, especially potentially big donors, in order to encourage potentially big donations? Well, no. Peter Wilderotter warns that, to sustain long-term relationships with donors, you have to convince them that they're making a savvy investment in a cause rather than just doing you a favor. Friendship is not the foundation for a sustainable business model.

A woman with a very famous last name once took an interest in Dress for Success. Her friends had seen us on *60 Minutes* and called her to say, "You've got to work with that organization. It's so you." She called and offered to take me to lunch. Of course, I went. She met me at a lovely, expensive spot where people drink cocktails at midday, midweek. The lunch lasted two hours. She asked me about the organization and about me, and then for the next ninety minutes she told me about herself, her troubled life, and the man she was dating. It was awkward, but the jewelry around her neck alone could have helped us dress thousands of women for interviews, for jobs where they would earn what she spent in an hour at Barneys. She never came to our offices, but at her request we did have three more dinners. Finally she told me to come by her apartment to pick up a check. When I arrived, she greeted me at the door in a robe and said, "Thank goodness! I had my breasts redone [for the third time], and I'm not sure they are even. Will you please look?" And she started unwrapping gauze.

At that point I shut my eyes, put my hands in the air, and practically screamed, "I'm so not qualified to judge that! Please. I really think I should go." She handed me an envelope, and I left. Quickly. I sent a nice, if overly formal, thank-you note for the $10,000, and I never heard from her again.

The whole nutty incident taught me a few lessons. Never meet with a potential donor anywhere but an office or a formal public

setting. Be friendly, but don't become the shoulder for their personal problems. And should I ever have my breasts done, be sure to get them right the first time. I probably could have milked that woman for a lot more money, but that would have made me a grifter, and I'm just not that type of person. Nor do I have the time that it would require. Plus, as not-for-profit leaders will tell you, "friends" (fake or real) don't really give organizations big money. It's the people who really believe in the product or service who invest in it big-time.

Mixing work and friendship can cloud the purpose of the relationship. Sometimes it's easier to say no to a request when it comes from a friend, but sometimes it's more difficult to clearly evaluate a friend's work, request a change order, or question a price. And oftentimes befriending someone can make you respect their work product less, not more. Simply, there is a difference between being friendly and being friends. In a work environment, I suggest the former.

BE VERY SPECIFIC.

Adding a deadline to an ask—and explaining that deadline—is a form of specificity that provides a sense of urgency. You don't want to make it too radical ("I need this money by tomorrow at noon!") because that seems desperate, and you don't want it too distant ("Anytime before January 2012") either, because that seems arbitrary. A reasonable deadline conveys seriousness and professionalism: you've got a timetable, and you need to stick to it. A rational date-stamp feels studied and intentional.

We've learned to make very pointed asks of donors focused not only on timing but also on substance. The less specific we are, the less likely we are to get a yes. Zainab Salbi will ask a donor to help fund a specific program in a specific country that helps a specific number of women. On the WomenforWomen.org site, there is a permanent button that says "Sponsor a Woman Survivor of War." It costs $27 per month, and you can pick a region from a drop-down

list: Afghanistan, Bosnia and Herzegovina, Democratic Republic of Congo, Iraq, Kosovo, Nigeria, Rwanda, or Sudan.

You can make a passionate plea for people to help you save the whales or stop global warming, but if your plea isn't rooted in a detailed plan or remedy, with numbers and facts and even a time-line, it will seem a little pie-in-the-sky. Off the top of my head, I can think of thirteen women's cancer organizations—why should a donor choose yours? Data helps you make your case. Great data and concrete action plans make it harder to say no.

Part of the issue is that when you don't give specifics, you're forcing the donor to do the hard work of figuring out how to help. "Please help" isn't going to be as effective as "Please help by hosting a dinner for ten people during the first week of June." Without that specificity, they have no idea what exactly you want them to do. It's left to the imagination, and when you are making a pitch, imagina-tion is not often going to be your friend. Specificity puts your request in the realm of the concrete and the possible. And if they say no, you have a starting point for negotiation. On the other hand, if they say a blanket no to "please help," you've got no additional asks.

As I sat in the meeting of that unnamed ginormous company, I imagined that the senior marketing person would soon be making a call to Yahoo: *We're launching a campaign in Q1, and we need you to build the platform for it. It's not going to be complicated. We don't need much. Will you do it?*

Underselling something, and then speaking in such sweeping terms, may be effective sometimes, but doesn't it create ill will over the long term? I'm a believer in always being honest and specific. I want someone to know what he or she has said yes to and to be 111 percent into it.

ASK FOR SOMETHING OTHER THAN MONEY.

I know we call it "fund-raising," but the most effective not-for-profits don't limit their fund-raising to asking for funds. We ask for refer-

rals, for volunteers, for product contributions, for advice. It's not that we don't want money—oh, do we want money!—but sometimes the best way to get free milk is to ask for a bowl of cereal.

I'll use an analogy that everyone will understand. Getting advice is like reaching first base, as everyone has advice to give, and getting big money is like reaching third. But enlisting a donor's time is a home run, because they run through all those other bases to get there, and they stay. Maybe the greatest not-for-profit leader at understanding the importance of this point is Barack Obama.

The Obama presidential campaign nailed this concept. The opening page of the Obama website featured a very important ask: Declare your support. Visitors were encouraged to register with the site but were not solicited for money. The key to this ask was that people visiting the site are obviously interested in the campaign, and their interest should be harnessed just as enthusiastically as—but cleverly, *before*—their money. Once the Obama campaign procured people's e-mail addresses, they were able to continue the ask. The campaign managers hooked supporters on Facebook and by text message updates, all of which were critical to the campaign, although they never once asked for money directly. Of the 14 million e-mails collected over the campaign, the majority did not yield donations. It's important to convey to supporters that you appreciate their support, not just their Gs. Most important, you can put a price on a donation, but people's time and non-financial support is invaluable. Asking for the latter demonstrates an understanding of the concept and will yield some great, often unpredictable returns.

At Dress for Success, our first ask to people was for their gently worn suits. Many women felt something deeply emotional and accessible about our request. A woman could donate a suit—maybe one she was wearing when she landed a key promotion—and know that another woman would be wearing it to a job interview that could transform her life. It's a much deeper connection than just handing over a check. It's like a giant virtual closet, one woman sharing with another.

One of the big secrets at Dress for Success is that we always had enough size 6 suits to clothe the population of a small nation, but (at least while I was there) we never turned away a single suit donor. Why? Because giving women the opportunity to contribute suits was the entry point; eventually, we hoped, they would become financial donors, volunteer personal shoppers, and ambassadors.

The point that may translate most easily to the for-profit sector is that asking for something other than money flatters your potential donor. If you want their smarts and their expertise, their introductions or their networks, you're tacitly acknowledging their status in a way that chasing their cash doesn't. You're making it appear that they're even *more* valuable to you than they expected. And it's not a ploy. As noted in other chapters, they *are* more valuable to you than you expected.

MAKE IT COOL.

Crunch, crunch, crunch. I know people think the not-for-profit sector is all granola, aging hippies, and crunchy vegans. Don't let the prevalence of Birkenstocks fool you! The not-for-profit sector understands trends, and we understand fashion. (For the record, I don't own any Birkenstocks, and I'm a registered Independent.) I don't mean fashion as in the latest thing that Marc Jacobs sent down the runway or the hottest bag, the cost of which could probably fund my organization for at least a month. By fashion, I mean patterns and fads and cycles of hot-or-not. I mean we know how to position our cause as the super-groovy thing of the moment.

There's power in prestige, in being seen as cool, and nobody in the not-for-profit sector understands this better than David Saltzman. For the last decade he has been executive director of the Robin Hood Foundation, which, in keeping with its name, takes from the rich and gives to the poor of New York City. Founded in the 1980s by a group of hedge fund managers and other investing types who wanted to do good, the group has a board of directors

that could be a finance geek's dream dinner party from billion-aires Paul Tudor Jones and George Soros to media mogul Harvey Weinstein.

The group does host a real-life dream dinner party, an annual New York City event that has become legendary for the entertainment. (The Who reunited there one year, Led Zeppelin another.) One recent dinner raised $72 million. (That was not a typo.) At one point during the party, David asked the audience, "Does anyone want to donate $1 million?" Sixteen hands went up. The live auction has become a friendly forum for hedge fund types to prove they had a good year, as they try to "win" the right to spend four days at Deepak Chopra's house with Madonna and Gwyneth. (Yes. Robin Hood is an organization where last names are optional.) Oh, and that auction item sold for a cool few hundred grand.

Does the foundation do good work? Yes. Many people credit it with helping turn around some of the city's toughest schools. And it has had an effect on illiteracy and homelessness as well, by funneling millions upon millions of dollars to organizations that could never throw such a party themselves. But this good work isn't why they raise so much money; it's because they're super-groovy. Could anyone raise $72 million in one night if Weird Al Yankovic were the evening's entertainment and the hot auction item were a free membership to the local gym? Robin Hood would never have such success if they weren't so darned H-O-T. Well, for hedge fund types anyway.

Don't snicker at Robin Hood. Its genius is that it taps its constituency's desire to be seen as cool (for giving lots of money) and to feel cool (by association with everyone else in the room). It's a mega version of many other charity events. Most people with a pulse want to be part of the action. So you send your $500 and suffer through yet another evening of salmon, overcooked asparagus, and disappointing dinner rolls. Admit it—you're a sucker for this stuff. It works. So why not copy these tactics in the for-profit world?

The tactic of capitalizing on people's desire to be the cool kid in the room isn't restricted to not-for-profits. In fact, we took

it from Molly Ringwald movies. The popular kid has the best car and the coolest house (and parents who go away a lot). Some companies understand this. I mean, T-Mobile sells cell phone service, and that's not sexy. But put a smoldering Catherine Zeta-Jones in your advertisements, and you're oozing cool. Or consider red pistachios. These nuts are actually born a dull beige. According to Eagle Ranch, a manufacturer of pistachios who doesn't use dyes, pistachios were originally dyed red to cover up blemishes and make them look pretty. People like pretty foods. Red stands out. The nuts sold. Those green pistachios and your green pistachio ice cream? Also dye. Face it, you've been sold a beige nut, thanks to the addition of food coloring. Selling a cool experience is an amazingly effective way to move product.

OFFER OPTIONS.

It's very easy for a potential donor to say no to one direct ask. But when presented with multiple options, people usually pick one.

The ASPCA presents a whole slew of options to potential donors. You can help by adopting a cat, a dog, or anything with four legs. Within those categories you could adopt Ying Yang the "go-getter dog," while someone who is more a party animal could go for Smoke, the dog the ASPCA dubs "the life of the party." Someone looking at the ASPCA website probably already loves animals. And chances are, if they show you ten cute, furry ones, you'll fall in love with at least one and become a sponsor.

At DoSomething.org we try to create flexibility for the payment of donations as possible. One person might want to pay equal amounts for twelve months. Another person—a sole proprietor, perhaps—would rather send us a check only in months where his quarterly taxes aren't due. That's fine, whatever works. A willingness to tailor payments to an individual's particular situation makes the ask that much more attractive.

Payment options and sponsorship types are the most obvious

form of variety. Smart not-for-profits also tailor-make volunteer opportunities for people's availability, preferences, and skill sets.

More companies might think like Burger King. Their entire platform is "Have it your way." And especially if you're targeting a youth market, you absolutely need to consider how those kids can customize your product or service. This generation has grown up with "grande soy frappuccinos with whip, no drizzle," playlists instead of albums, and nineteen hundred TV channels. Choice is a way of life, a basic assumption, like air. How does your company cope with this reality?

KEEP IT REAL—AND KEEP IT ON THE HUMAN LEVEL.

The experience of donating, like the experience of buying almost anything, can be sterile. Sometimes you write that check, and you don't really have any idea where that money is going. Who's receiving it? How are they using it? What is the real effect of that money?

What successful not-for-profits do is make clear the real-world effects of the donations they receive. Nobody does this better than DonorsChoose.org, which is clear that the surcharge on your donation goes to cover organizational costs. And when you visit the DonorsChoose.org site and respond to a sixth-grade class in Little Rock, Arkansas, requesting $50 for school supplies, you know that that sixth-grade class in Little Rock will be receiving your $50 for school supplies. Having the teachers ask for funding for specific purposes personalizes the request, conferring upon it a tangible as well as a heartfelt aspect that takes giving to a new level.

Smart not-for-profits have also learned to take numbers outside the realm of abstraction and translate them into the everyday, which is something that many for-profits should certainly be able to do easily. Take, for instance, the staff at charity: water, which has done the math and figured out exactly how much it costs to provide one person with clean drinking water for life: $20. With a few simple cal-

culations and some good data, they have taken an impossibly huge problem and boiled it down into something we can understand—and that we feel can be conquered. They have translated from gibberish into English.

This number is now the centerpiece of charity: water's ask. Every e-mail includes it. Every item of merchandise has this number worked into the cost. *The cost of this sweatshirt can help one person; buy one $20 bottle of water, save a life; this e-card can give one person clean water for life.* And perhaps most important, charity: water makes every effort to show the impact of $20, because the worst thing that could happen would be for donors to get the impression that the number is just a marketing gimmick. So it posts pictures from the field of children helped, and it creates Google maps showing the spread of the organization's work.

The key here is to humanize fund-raising and marketing. That is a secret to not-for-profit success, and I think it translates very well to the for-profit sector. People respond to requests for money when they're approached by people they like, people who are like them, and people whom they trust. We use humor, empathy, and shared values to raise money. We acknowledge that prospective donors have got both smarts and hearts, and we appeal to both. Charity: water's tactic was all about appealing to logic and reason—look how little it costs to save one person!—so let me share with you a case study that illustrates the power of reaching for the heartstrings and tugging a little.

Veronica Colondam runs an Indonesian social enterprise called the Loving the Nation's Children Foundation. It operates under a hybrid business model, deriving some revenue from the manufacture of a robotic toy animal but most of it from donations. The organization's purpose is to provide and expand educational opportunities for street children. Although educational programs are irrefutably important—everyone everywhere these days knows that it's a good thing for kids to go to school—convincing people to contribute to a program that doesn't yield instantaneous results is difficult. It's hard to convince people to invest when they might not see the returns for years and years.

Veronica has overcome this obstacle mightily, by appealing not to logic (education is good!) but to the emotion (childhood education is what every parent would desire for their child). Veronica has no shortage of emotional stories that she can deploy on behalf of her cause. She especially likes to speak of Neneng Julia, a homeless girl who used to sell snacks and tea by the side of the road. Veronica's program gave this ambitious and entrepreneurial kid some direction and stability. Upon graduation, Neneng landed a scholarship to further her studies in hairdressing and has forged a good life for herself. Today Neneng is back with Veronica, volunteering her story (and her hairdressing skills!) to other students at the center. She loves her job, and she delights in passing her good fortune on to the younger generation of underprivileged in the very place she grew up.

When I asked Veronica about her fund-raising strategy, she was frank. The bottom line, she said, is that "parents cannot deny their children." These stories stir raw human emotion. In most cases, the parents can't help but be touched—and give. She has found that the way to people's pockets is through their hearts.

Not-for-profits know that by bringing a donation to life, we can create a stronger connection with donors. For-profits can—and have tried to—do the same through advertising and marketing. You may not be able to achieve the same level of emotion, but the key is to keep it real. Bring your product or service down to a human level. Find the emotion in it.

My favorite for-profit example? OnStar. It's an in-car communication system that is overwhelmingly used for procuring directions. But the emotional pull—and the advertisements—demonstrates its usefulness in emergency situations. A mom has a flat on the side of the road, and the OnStar operator sends help . . . and some crackers for the cute kid in the backseat. Now it's not a communication technology. OnStar is a company that cares about people and makes their lives better.

BE SHAMELESS.

We not-for-profit types love our cause so much that we think everyone ought to be part of it. We think we are doing you a favor, saving you from your own ignorance or boredom or lack of purpose. So we tend to be a bit shameless. I've watched the founder of YouthAIDS, Kate Roberts, work a room. She walks right up to the most powerful people on the planet, smiles, introduces herself, shakes their hand, and asks them to help YouthAIDS with something. Sometimes she doesn't even bother with the handshake.

Kate and I once attended a World Economic Forum meeting together in China. More than a thousand important people from around the world were present. They were as influential and as powerful as their outfits were unimaginative—mostly men, they were all in dark suits with white shirts and super-boring ties that you'd never want to give your dad for Father's Day. At one dinner the CEO of the largest mobile phone provider in China addressed the group and then took a few questions from the floor. Kate stood up, smiled politely, and thanked him for his remarks. She then told the room that AIDS is ravaging the planet and that governments and foundations would not be able to stem the epidemic without the help of private business, so would he please consider contributing one penny to her cause, for every call made? Half the people in the room were in awe at her gutsiness, and the other half were in shock that our speaker had been put on the spot so publicly. He gracefully told her that he would love to help, and she should contact his office directly. I can only compare Kate's style to how I imagine a Mormon missionary might approach a convention of agnostics.

God bless her—and replicate her. My point isn't to show that Kate is a one-woman whirlwind, which she is. Not-for-profit people are often missing that shy gene, the thing that makes a normal person think twice and then stop himself. Instead, we believe we're on the side of the angels, and so we ask anyone and everyone we come in contact with for help. My argument is that we all ought to have such chutzpah. Find your inner Kate.

Have you ever looked back on a missed opportunity with regret? I don't think Kate has. So the next time you are at a restaurant and you see Michael Dell across the room, walk up to him and tell him about your computer thingamabob.

REPEAT YOURSELF.

Not-for-profits that are savvy about fund-raising usually recognize the value of repetition. Not-for-profits that are savvy about fund-raising usually recognize the value of repetition.

We've essentially updated that old salesman's credo, *Don't take no for an answer.* Our version? *Don't take an answer for an answer.* If someone doesn't make a contribution the first time you ask them, they might make one the second or third time. And, if they do say yes the first time, you probably didn't ask for enough. Either way, we don't settle for the first answer, always pushing for something more. (Remember in the Introduction I warned you about this: we go to eleven.)

Not-for-profit people hear *no* a lot. We ourselves assume that nineteen out of every twenty foundation applications we submit will be rejected. But we don't stop asking. Which is why you get so much mail from organizations such as Make-A-Wish, which relies heavily on direct-mail solicitations. They typically send the letters every eight weeks, believing that eventually you'll relent and send some money. Some people even forget that they already did. Bonus!

BELIEVE THAT SILENCE SPEAKS VOLUMES.

Sometimes the most important thing I have to say is nothing at all. If you want your audience to feel something, you've got to give them the time to think. Let them fill the hole in the air with their own voice. Let them try to tell you that no, they really don't want to help you.

Smart sales clerks don't just talk. And they don't just listen. They're okay with those "pause" moments. They allow people to look at the watch on their wrist and daydream and imagine that outfit. Silence makes people squirm—and filling the void with a *yes* is easier than a *no*.

SAY THANK YOU.

I need to follow my own advice above and repeat this one over and over and over. Gratitude is the cheapest and easiest way to keep a donor happy. By law, not-for-profits have to provide receipts to donors for their tax records. Most of these letters are boilerplate, but they don't have to be so dull. At Dress for Success, we sent brightly colored postcards that said, "Thank you. Thank you. Thank you. Because of your contribution of suits, women were able to attend job interviews feeling confident and looking dressed for success." Our thank-you note connected the contribution to the purpose. Arriving by hot pink postcard, it was unpredictable and fun, memorable and colorful—and it saved us money on postage.

Of course, the best thank-you isn't a postcard or an engraved piece of Lucite or an "I totally owe you lunch" date. The best thank-you is a heartfelt personal phone call, and given the right calling plan, it shouldn't cost you more than a few dimes. But do people at ginormous companies make these calls? Or do they send out a mug with their corporate logo on it instead?

If what I'm advocating is brownnosing, then not-for-profit leaders must all be born nose first, the better for the sun to turn it deep, deep brown. But I actually think that saying thank you, authentically and consistently, is a skill that we learn at not-for-profits because we are so genuinely grateful to people who give to us and yet receive practically nothing in return. It is absolutely true that without their support we'd be nowhere. So we tell them so.

Ami Dar did this just the other day with a donor who happened to mention Idealist.org in her blogpost. He sent her a heartfelt, per-

sonal e-mail telling her that he was grateful to have such a wonderful advocate out there. He took the time to share with her his vision for the future of the organization because he hoped she would be a big part of it. She responded by sending him a check for $500,000. Hey, it happens—people do love to get notes, especially handwritten letters.

ELEVEN QUESTIONS TO GET YOU STARTED:
Do More by Asking Smart

I could have included in the title of this chapter the word *sales* or *fund-raising*. But I didn't. Everyone in a company—not just the biz dev guys or the sales team—needs to refine their art of asking for stuff, money, and help.

Something else I didn't do in this chapter is talk about leveraging power in order to land a *yes*. It's often the first instinct of someone who wonders, How can I make my employee, or customer, or Yahoo do something for me? All my suggestions have been things that *we* do, practice, and repeat, not demand or just expect as a matter of position. You may find that you attract more bees with a handful of honey than with a clenched fist. Try it. Ask yourself:

1. Before you ask someone for something, do you think about why that person might say yes or no?

2. Do you plan before you ask? Or do you wing it? Do you just go through the motions of the old routine?

3. Are you so friendly that it's easy to say no to you? Are you so friendly that you aren't taken seriously? Or conversely, are you so cold that nobody wants to do you a favor?

4. Do your requests for help or money (or both) have clear deadlines and expectations?

5. When is the last time you told someone thank you without being prompted?

6. When you ask, do you give options to your vendors, employees, co-workers, and customers?

7. Have you ever left a sale on the table? What stopped you from making the ask?

8. What do you do when someone tells you *no*? Have you ever turned a *no* into a *yes*? How did you do it? Can you do it again?

9. If you were in an elevator with Oprah (or Bill Gates, or someone else who could be helpful to your company), what would you say? (FYI, it's not a very tall building. You've only got thirty seconds.)

10. Can you turn your beige request into something red or green? Is there a more fun way to position your request?

11. Why are you asking this person? What do you have in common?

5

DO MORE FOR CUSTOMERS

AS I SAT THERE in the ginormous company's fancy conference room, it occurred to me that everything they said about their target market was a ploy to get them to take an action—to consume, to buy, to transfer money into said ginormous company's increasingly ginormous (but maybe not enough) coffers. They expressed no genuine love for the customer. He was a target. She was a sitting duck. Customers apparently had no inherent value beyond what they were able to add to the ginormous company's bottom line and no purpose apart from keeping everyone in that room employed. The customer would have been completely irrelevant, except that the ad campaigns being created needed an audience and the product being manufactured needed someone to buy it—and then buy some more. But why?

Why? is the question we ask all the time in the not-for-profit world, but we're not asking it about ourselves. We're thinking about it from the perspective of the other. I know that sounds all hoity-toity—

what normal person speaks of "the other"?—but let me put it another way. We're deeply concerned about the customer and about customer service. On my planet, we truly believe in being other-centric. Other people really matter, more than I know how to explain, but let me give it a try.

People often donate to not-for-profits for a tangible reason: that tax-deduction receipt. But they always donate to a particular not-for-profit for intangible ones. Perhaps it's that they get a chance to feel part of a community. Or that they have the sense that they're making a difference, especially in a field that they care about, be it disaster relief or fighting homelessness or saving cats. They enjoy giving money to an organization that reflects their beliefs and values, so they tithe at church or send a check to Catholic Charities. They choose to participate in meaningful and enjoyable activities and want others, particularly the less fortunate, to enjoy those as well, so they give to the Fresh Air Fund or the Hole in the Wall Gang.

Instead of receiving in return a quality product or terrific service or a low, low price, they receive an intangible—a feeling, an experience, a membership. Such returns on their investment can't be measured in traditional terms. There is no metric for "gross domestic spiritual product" or "net emotional-asset value." But anyone who has experienced such intangibles knows how powerful and how motivational they are.

Why do these intangibles matter so much? Because that donor could give to a gazillion other charities very similar to yours, but they picked yours. It's the same in the for-profit marketplace. There are very few products that have true monopolies. For-profits, too, have to compete, and they have to do so largely on the basis of the intangibles they offer. For-profits, too, can use a little of that love. Product parity, cost-effective competition, and fleeting costumer loyalty make it increasingly difficult to make money by selling purely on price or value. Companies that want to lock up customers for the long term have plenty to learn from the expertise and experience of not-for-profits that don't have much to trade on apart from their intangibles.

SEE PEOPLE FIRST, BUYERS SECOND.

Not-for-profits don't see donors as walking pocketbooks or wallets with legs and arms attached. We work hard to view them in terms of their human traits. It's not that we're oblivious to the amount they contribute or their potential lifetime value to us—in fact, we've got software and staff members tracking every one of those stats— but we are just as concerned with the wide variety of motivations that drive each donation, because that's going to help us connect with and build a relationship with that person. An extensive range of dreams and disappointments, experiences and emotions, inspire people to give time, money, and energy.

Let's look at some of the very human characteristics, traits, virtues, and woes that drive people to make donations, whether of their cash or of their caring.

Some people are motivated by guilt. Often they feel guilty about something that has happened in their lives, something they did that contributed to a social problem or even something they failed to do to remedy it. And so their guilt inspires them to want to make it right, to atone for it, in sort of a modern-day version of a biblical sin offering.

Other people may be driven by a quest for goodness. Their membership in a group—it could be a church or a synagogue or a country club or a sorority—may motivate them to think and act in a certain way. Much of their group may be moved to act by shared values—we do something because we are X or Y. But one subset of this group is compelled not by its values but by peer pressure, by the need to be seen by their social cohort as an integral part of the group that does X or Y.

Empathy can be a major source of social action. Think of natural disasters and the strong emotions that can arise as someone watches the news on television of thousands of people left homeless by a cyclone or children orphaned by war. Many people are stirred to care about those who suffer from a problem that the not-for-profit is attempting to address.

A related emotion is anger, a kind of "we're mad as hell and we're not going to take it anymore" fury that can often effectively lead to charitable involvement. Fury at a societal situation or perceived injustice can lead people to take a stand with their time, money, contacts, and connections. Righteous anger has spawned revolutions.

Possibly my least favorite driver of giving, but one no less powerful, is ego. People like to look good. They want to feel like big shots. They want to brag to their friends that they gave X number of dollars to their alma mater or to the opera. They want to show off the painting they bought at the silent auction. They want to see their names on the wall of a new library or art museum. Really, they want other people to see their names on that wall.

The point of listing these motivations isn't to compare them in terms of karmic value or relative moral worth. The point is to understand the spectrum on which we all live, so that for-profits can get, as effective not-for-profits have, (a) a strong understanding of these motivations and (b) the ability to sense which one is in play in a particular situation. Does this make not-for-profit people kind of like lay psychologists and pseudoshrinks? Absolutely. We're trying to read minds and hearts all the time. We want to know, *And how do you feel about that?*

Among consumers, it goes without saying, this range of emotion, this psychological spectrum, is constantly at play in any setting where a buyer has to make a choice. Consider automobiles. Some guy may buy a Cadillac because his father always wanted one—consciously or not, he's honoring his dad by his car choice. Another individual may think of herself as a Subaru woman—tough, independent-minded, free-spirited. A third may buy a Mercedes convertible because she wants a car that makes her feel young and sexy and alive—because she recently beat cancer and wants to celebrate the wind in her hair. A fourth may love music and will buy the car with the best stereo system. A fifth may buy the Ford Escape Hybrid because she wants to buy American (U.S.A.! U.S.A.!), but she also wants to do something good for the environment, and put-

ting her small children in an SUV just seems safer. And those are just the examples from my own family! (Yes, I'm sure you guessed it. I'm the Ford Escape Hybrid.)

The smart not-for-profit—and the smart for-profit—learns how to mine those preferences and predilections. Tons of people are trying to compete on price and value. Not everyone is acknowledging the human aspects of the decision-making process. By giving them appropriate respect, we gain a competitive advantage over our rivals. By seeing donors as people, not as ATMs, we help maximize their value to us—as people who can give more than just money . . . and of course as people who can give money.

REMEMBER THAT CUSTOMERS LIKE TO BE PART OF SOMETHING BIGGER.

In Chapter 1, I said that employees like to feel they're part of something big. Well, so do customers.

Not-for-profits are known for holding all sorts of fund-raising events that allow people to participate actively. Instead of just writing a check, those who want to give can run, walk, or bike; they can bid in silent auctions or live ones while eating bland chicken breasts at gala dinners; they can participate in parades; they can take part in various competitions. Such events go beyond fund-raising. They also cultivate a sense of belonging. They provide a sense of inclusion and affiliation—especially if everyone gets a free T-shirt!—binding people to a not-for-profit in a way that goes beyond a cold financial exchange.

Ever seen one of those thermometers that measure total giving? You find them at charity events as well as on websites where walk-athon participants are tracking how much they have raised toward their goal. Maybe a United Way drive has a goal of $5 million, and the colored in bits of the meter show that $3 million is already in hand. Or maybe Aunt Susan is going to do that 5K run to support multiple sclerosis research and has set her target at $250. Big goal or

small, you really want to help reach that goal. You want to be part of the team behind the success. Often people check repeatedly to see whether the target has been reached—and sometimes they give a little more. The appeal is that you can visualize your contribution as part of a bigger effort. The group, the army of supporters, turns out to be more than the sum of its parts.

A similar motivation propels some donors to make matching pledges: if you donate one dollar by X date, Mr. and Mrs. Y have pledged to give one dollar too! Sometimes they throw in a deadline; when my local public radio station does one of its regular fund drives, for instance, they'll say that some big donor is going to match gifts only in the next thirty minutes—which adds a sense of collective urgency to the group mission. Or for every ten hours of volunteer time you give to the Red Cross, your friend Jim Smith will donate $100. It inspires you to do more, and it inspires him to contribute more, because you are in it together. Your donation—of time and/or money—has even more of an effect because someone is partnering with you.

I confess I thought it was somehow cool that McDonald's changed its signs from "millions served" to "billions served." I know, I know—it's a for-profit, and those billions of customers probably didn't need that supersized Coke or the large french fries instead of the medium, and you may not share my good feelings about seeing it. But the point is that more companies should tap into that spirit. Instead of issuing coupon codes for customers to get 10 percent off, how about issuing one that works only when they bring a friend? People today are constantly talking about data-driven strategies, so how about putting some of that data to good use and doing the time-honored "one-thousandth customer served here" celebration? If you can't afford the balloons, how about just singing a song and shouting "Whoohoo"? It won't cost you a penny, and everyone in the store will feel appreciated, not just that customer turning red at the cash register.

The Millennium Promise is committed to tackling world poverty by 2015. It's impossible for one person to imagine conquer-

ing it within five years—or ever. But it is empowering, even a little goosebump-inducing, to picture oneself as part of a mass of angry humanity striving for this colossal goal of justice. You know what? The Millennium Promise is bait for prowling donors. No, not because Angelina Jolie is on the letterhead (although that doesn't hurt), but because people like to be part of a big movement. Who doesn't want to end world hunger? That's such a broad, positive, big goal that it doesn't alienate anyone. It's a winner. Why do winning teams have more fans? We like to jump on that long tail.

CELEBRATE LOCAL ELEMENTS.

Localizing returns can be a powerful tactic. We're living in the era of the locavore—and I'm convinced that people don't want just to eat local, they want to live local. They want to feel good about their communities. They want to improve them. They want to feel proud of them. They have loyalty to the area. They want it to be cleaner, safer, more literate, and healthier. Whether the reason is self-interest or community spirit—and surely it's a little bit of both—some highly successful not-for-profits have built their success on a community strategy that taps into local pride.

One of my favorite examples is KaBOOM!—an organization that believes in the power of play and constructs wacky, colorful playgrounds and jungle gyms all around the country. The group could, if it wanted to, work with city government, plop their projects down in a park, and leave. But this isn't how it operates, because KaBOOM! was founded on the principle that playgrounds are about community. In fact, it makes a point of rallying individual communities around a local goal. By funding and building playgrounds for deserving children in socioeconomically disadvantaged areas, KaBOOM! communicates that it is working with the people of the community to beautify and improve their neighborhood, their locale. By involving local children and families in the design, planning, and building of their own playground, KaBOOM! is en-

suring that it isn't seen as an outsider bigfooting its way into town, imposing something on the community. Rather, it's a partnership with local individuals who are sharing in the process.

You can see from KaBOOM!'s method that this commitment isn't just a matter of philosophy but real, integrated practice. No organization that just wanted to pay lip service to community would ever go to such lengths. As soon as KaBOOM! secures a funding partner for a new project, it hosts a Design Day bringing together all the members of the community to brainstorm. Kids come and sketch their dream play-spaces. The adults talk about managing the assets that KaBOOM! is bringing to the project, and they strategize about how to exploit locally available resources. After approximately two months of planning and arranging all the proper equipment— and of course, food and drink—the group members reunite at the building site for one day of intense, roll-up-your-sleeves work. Volunteers from the funding partners share hammers with community members, and the team erects the vision they have built in their minds and their discussions and sketched out on paper. Clearly KaBOOM! could roll into communities and erect playgrounds without any local involvement. Would kids play there? Of course. But the founders of KaBOOM! recognize that involving community members is more than just getting free labor. It fosters community ownership of a project as a way of instilling pride in it and maximizing the likelihood that it will be well loved, well used, and well maintained for years afterward. This model also strengthens communities and creates momentum for future improvement projects. The volunteers stand on the site of their finished playgrounds marveling not only "look what we did" but "look what we can do!"

Another, less obvious manifestation of this concept comes from the Christopher and Dana Reeve Foundation. The Reeve Foundation could simply channel its energy into funding research that might eventually lead to a cure for spinal cord conditions and diseases. It's important work. It's worthy work. But the organization doesn't—and shouldn't—stop there. It has created an online community where people with spinal injuries, as well as their friends

and families, can support one another. The site is a place to share advice, collect resources for lobbying on the related issues, list the latest advances in the field, and commiserate. It has no zip code. Most of the people may never meet in person. Yet thanks to the foundation that conceived it and built the infrastructure that allows these people to meet, it's a bona fide, active community.

There are for-profits that foster community. A few do it particularly well. For instance, Coors Brewing has always made the most of being a Colorado company; it has built that brand image in its marketing, and it has thrived on loyalty from its home staters. By advertising itself as New York City's "hometown airline" and investing in local community efforts, JetBlue has earned a certain amount of loyalty among New Yorkers.

But on the whole, I sense a reluctance among national brands to cultivate a local image, probably because they fear being pigeonholed as a small-scale or regional (*oh! the horror!*) brand. What they don't realize is that a smart company can easily be simultaneously local and national—and even global. Many companies are identified as "local" to a particular, well, locale—such as Ford with Detroit and Microsoft with Seattle (or Redmond, if you want to be super-nitpicky about it). They are still globally recognized brands with vast customer bases.

The point is that companies are actually missing a significant opportunity by neglecting their local affiliation. It wouldn't be tough to provide local communities some incentives to buy a hometown product. For instance, *everyone* in Camden, New Jersey, should be buying Campbell's Soup. Companies should also construct loyalty programs wherever they have offices, not just near their headquarters. Ginormous companies have hundreds or even thousands of manufacturing facilities, branch offices, and service centers throughout the world. Why not appeal to each community's sense of pride? Why not cultivate some of that pride—and allow the halo to envelop your company?

MAKE THE SHIFT FROM NICE TO IMPORTANT.

In the not-for-profit world, we hold this truth to be self-evident: that people give to causes that are important, not just causes that are nice. If you want someone to give up a Saturday in the summer to walk for your cause or to write you a check that could fund a kid's college education, they won't do it if they think you're just nice. You've got to be important. And so does your cause.

It isn't a matter of mere branding. It's about the effectiveness of your organization and about maximizing your opportunity to tap into donors and volunteers. How far they will go for you depends largely on how valuable your product is to them. Is it something that will compel them to do more than the minimum? Let's look at it this way: to be a not-for-profit fighting illiteracy in a number of different countries is nice, because illiteracy is bad. But imagine how much more powerful it would be—how *important*—to improve education so much in one country that it essentially single-handedly *ends* illiteracy. Being Important (and that capital *I* is intentional) requires a purpose with a measurable effect.

Much of importance has to do with perception, and that's where branding and communication do come in. Perception matters a lot, and some not-for-profits have done a great job of communicating excitement about their efforts. Using everything from sophisticated Web technology to old-fashioned public relations campaigns, they've made a strong case for being meaningful, important groups. Every arts and music program faces this challenge. In down economies, they are the first programs to be cut. They're deemed expendable, optional, frills. But the Alvin Ailey American Dance Theater has done a masterful job of making the shift from nice to important by stressing the "crucial social role" the company plays in African American heritage and in uniting people of all races, ages, and backgrounds. Simply, it's not just about dance. It's about cultural preservation. It's about antidiscrimination. It's about education.

To some extent, not-for-profits elevate themselves from nice to Important through a vision, translated through the words of a charis-

matic leader. People easily fall under the spell of not-for-profit leaders who connect their cause to an important problem or moment. A man named Van Jones comes to mind. Best known for his brief stint as Obama's "Green Czar," Jones, who lives in Oakland, California, founded an organization called Green For All. Its purpose is to bring "green collar" jobs—from asbestos removal to weatherizing to planting community gardens—to low-income neighborhoods. The idea is that disadvantaged youths will be able to do these jobs and thereby become positive, not negative, elements in their communities. No matter what your political background (or views on Jones and his political persuasions), green jobs are a nice idea that becomes an Important idea when you understand the connection between environmental degradation and poverty. The secret to Green For All's success is the urgency—that sense of importance and imminence—that the organization manages to project.

Green For All presses the point that it's crucial not only to preserve our planet and ensure environmental progress but also to provide real jobs for urban youth. That two-pronged approach is provocative and compelling. There is nothing warm and fuzzy about Green For All's vision. Unless we have a strong plan to protect our environment, our planet is toast. Without a healthy working class, the economy will falter further.

Going that extra step from nice to important is something that many companies, whether for-profit or not, can do. Is your product simply a nice thing for your customers to have or use or try? Or have you managed to convince them that it's important? Have you even convinced *yourself* that it's important? Your product may be important to your customers because it is nutritious or will make them more attractive. Or maybe your product is a commodity, something interchangeable in a competitive space. In that case, you might consider borrowing importance by partnering with a third party. That's called cause marketing.

PARTNER FOR A PURPOSE.

In the not-for-profit sector, we joke that the biggest intangible we offer is a front-row seat in heaven. But we don't have the lock on those seats. Not-for-profit companies never signed an exclusivity agreement, so believe it or not, for-profit companies can offer them too. You just have to know how.

A handful of companies understand this heavenly strategy; as I like to say, they have learned how to rock cause. American Express was first to enter the arena, back in the 1970s, when it attached its brand with the closely watched renovation of the Statue of Liberty. A portion of revenues from certain credit cards went to help save an American icon. The idea was that shopping became an act of patriotism. It was clever, and it worked—after all, I'm still writing about it.

Another example is Yoplait's "Save Lids to Save Lives" campaign, which began in 1998. It raises awareness of breast cancer and funds to fight it. The campaign has forged a link between the company, the disease, and the target market (women) that has not only greatly helped in the war against breast cancer but has also given Yoplait a leg up in its quest for more market share.

There is nothing explicitly warm and fuzzy about credit card companies (which annoyingly send me bills each month) or yogurt (which I eat instead of ice cream because I think I should). They are just articles of trade. They are products. They are commodities. I don't "love" them. But pair them with a cause? Now I'm feelin' something.

Am I just a sucker or does cause marketing work a spell on most people? Cone Inc., a leading agency in the cause-branding field, has studied these types of campaigns and proved their effectiveness. Cone's data show that two-thirds of people will switch from one brand to another if a "replacement" product or service of comparable value is associated with a cause. And here is the kicker: the cause doesn't even have to be something the consumer cares about. Almost any cause will do. Consumers seem to simply like the

idea that consumption has some sort of additional meaning beyond satisfying their needs and desires.

We've all seen the trend in the marketplace—with the rise of fair-trade goods, for instance—of people buying with their consciences. More and more consumers are choosing businesses that promote their green credentials or are affiliated with philanthropic endeavors. Cause-marketing partnerships are part of this trend, because they make customers feel good about their purchases.

I want to be clear about this: you can't just throw money at a cause and assume that it will optimize your success. Some big companies seem to believe that as long as they make a big deal about giving a lot of money to a cause—any cause—they'll reap the benefits. Macy's, for example, recently hosted Shop for a Cause Day. It did extensive promotion and publicity, providing information in its stores and running full-page advertisements in newspapers. The idea was that if customers bought something at Macy's on this special day, the company would give a percentage of the revenue to worthy causes. But Macy's didn't identify the causes by name in its advertising! It assumed that generic giving would suffice. Afterward the company claimed that the day had been a success, but I assert that it could and would have been even more successful if the company had chosen—and named—a few charities that were identifiably popular among its target demographics.

In the not-for-profit world, we know that you can't be a generic do-gooder and expect to have the most impact. The most successful not-for-profits don't just help—they pioneer. They carve out their own niches. They concoct innovative approaches to problems. They target neglected segments of the large cause market.

If you are going to create a sense of purpose for your brand by marrying it with a cause or organization, choose wisely. Pick something that resonates with your customer. Choose an organization that is excited to work with you on creative execution strategies. And have some specific impact in mind.

For the last three years Aéropostale, the international teen-focused clothing retailer, has partnered with DoSomething.org on a

very successful cause-marketing partnership to battle the persistent and growing problem of youth homelessness. One-third of all homeless people in the United States are under the age of eighteen. The first thing they request when reaching a shelter? Denim. Aéropostale and Do Something partnered to create a campaign called Teens for Jeans, which encourages young people to bring their gently used blue jeans (of any brand) to a local Aéropostale store. Do Something redistributes them to five hundred youth shelters nationwide.

I call this program a win-win-win. Do Something is happy because we collected more than six hundred thousand pairs of jeans for homeless kids in just three weeks. Aéropostale is happy for that same reason, and it's even happier that all those people had to come to their stores to drop off their contributions. Some of them even stuck around to buy something. And the customer is happy knowing she made a difference in someone else's life, cleaned out her closet, and maybe bought an awesome new pair of jeans while she was there.

Of course, a whole class of for-profit companies have made causes not just a marketing ploy but an essential part of how they function, what they make, how they spend their money, and where the profits go. These socially responsible companies include KIND, the fruit and nut bar, which is manufactured jointly by Arabs and Israelis. The company is partially owned by OneVoice, which works for a peaceful solution in the Middle East. TOMS Shoes sells shoes made from recycled materials and, for every pair sold, gives a pair to a person in impoverished, rural Africa. TOMS has been featured in popular American Express advertisements as the pinnacle of responsible for-profit entrepreneurship.

These types of companies are increasingly popular. And some are poised for great success, in large part because of their do-gooder nature. I'm not suggesting that every company pipe "Kumbaya" over the loudspeakers and put solar panels on the headquarter's roof—unless, that is, a good business case can be made for leading a sing-along or hooking up to a sustainable energy source.

The point is that people are overtly caring about the world

around them more than ever. Multiple demographic groups are emerging that value goodness over price, and they are making purchasing decisions based on those feelings. It's happening in surprising ways. The head of Waitrose supermarkets in the U.K. was shocked, for instance, when he looked at the numbers for his meat-department sales during the recession—overall volume was down, because people were buying less meat, but sales of humanely raised meat were up, because they were buying meat from the animals that had been treated well.

It's the growing population of that kind of consumer that is the best argument for changing the way you do business. I can't promise you that you'll feel better about yourself or that you'll find yourself invited to more parties or that you'll get one of those front-row seats in heaven. But I can say this: companies that do good are companies that are looking out for their bottom lines. Partner with a cause, not because it feels good, but because it's good for your business.

FOLLOW THE TOTE BAG PRINCIPLE.

People want stuff. Let's be honest, they especially want free stuff, a gift with a purchase, buy-one-get-one-free offers. In other words, people love extras. And there's a good business argument to be made for giving them what they want.

I once sold a $50,000 table for a charitable dinner to a billionaire. He wasn't able to attend the event himself, and so he sent some of his staff to enjoy the evening. But he did have one request: Would I please send him the gift bag? To be clear, this wasn't the famed Oscars gift bag, with its free mattresses and facials and four-day, three-night luxury getaways to the latest resort on the Mexican Riviera. My event was just another dinner in New York City, one of hundreds that riddle the social calendar every season, and the bag was, for its kind, pretty ordinary. It contained some shampoo samples, a key chain from a bank, a Nalgene water bottle bearing the logo of a local moving company, a copy of *Glamour* magazine that was

already on newsstands, and a pen with the organization's logo on it. Oh, and the bag itself was a canvas tote with the organization's logo splashed across it. To be honest, the billionaire could have afforded to buy three of the companies represented in the bag, and I think he was already the major shareholder in two of the others. But still, he was thrilled to receive his "free" gift bag.

Airlines (for the most part a "nonprofit" business these days, it seems) used to understand the value of intangibles. When you flew, you received all sorts of bonuses. Some of them were tangible—kids received airline wings that they could pin to their shirts, while adults received free minibottles of liquor. Everyone received a decent meal, served with a smile by a stewardess. A rack near the lavatories had postcards and stationery; some airlines even mailed them for you without charge. People were given tours of the cockpit. Stewardesses responded courteously and promptly to requests. Seats were relatively wide and comfortable. Some planes had lounge areas. There were pillows and blankets in abundance, as well as piles of free magazines—not just the airline's own but *Time* and *Newsweek* and *People* and *Sports Illustrated* and *Vogue*—to get you through the flight. In short, people received more than transportation when they bought their tickets—they got an experience and freebies that, sometimes subtly and sometimes not, worked together to build customer satisfaction and hence brand loyalty. Now we're lucky if we manage to get a flight that just lands on time.

Estée Lauder gets the Tote Bag Principle. The cosmetics company is constantly offering gifts with purchase—free mascara or a lovely cosmetics travel bag. Could the consumer afford to buy these things? Certainly. Is she essentially buying these things, by purchasing the requisite amount to trigger the gift? Of course. But it feels like it's free. And free feels goooood.

Corporations can offer symbolic items to customers. They are often proud to make a purchase from Nike, Apple, Starbucks, and other companies with a robust brand. Providing them with an additional item besides the product purchased gives them a tangible extra, but it's the intangible value of that premium that matters. All

those companies used to give out logo stickers, for instance. That's an inexpensive way to give the feeling of a bonus while spreading the brand even further.

WELCOME THEM TO THE CLUB.

In Chapter 3, I discussed how important it is to make sure that the people in your external networks—as well as those within your organization—feel that they belong. I can't emphasize enough how important this also is for your customers. You want and need them to feel like a member of a special club.

You can foster this sense of inclusion in all sorts of ways. Take these examples from not-for-profits.

- Thank-you notes from a celebrity associated with the not-for-profit, like Bette Midler's letters to those who support her public garden initiatives. People love flipping through their stack of bills to find the return address—from Bette!

- Specialty hospitals like Sloan-Kettering or organizations focused on a particular disease like the Christopher and Dana Reeve Foundation will host special question-and-answer events with thought leaders, researchers, and medical professionals.

- YouthAIDS and other organizations focused internationally create special tours for select groups of donors to travel abroad, with guided access.

One for-profit company that understands this really well is Build-A-Bear. This fast-growing company was founded in St. Louis in 1997 by Maxine Clark. It now has more than four hundred stores around the world—there's even one at Nationals Stadium in Washington, D.C., where you can build your very own fan bear. The chain has become known as *the* place where you create your own

stuffed animal, complete with clothing, accessories, and a birth cer-
tificate. What is brilliant about that birth certificate (which people
fill out themselves on computer terminals at the store) is that in en-
tering information about your bear, you are signing up for the mail-
ing list. On your animal's birthday you receive a birthday card—a
signal of your (or your bear's?) membership in a special society.

Lululemon athletica sells yoga wear to women and men. It also
offers free yoga classes right there in the store or sometimes in a
nearby park, and every lululemon store has a community board of-
fering a space for people to post local healthy events.

Foot Locker hosts special "insiders only" events when it launches
limited-edition shoes. This practice encourages consumer loyalty,
enhances brand strength in the customer's mind as "the only" place
where you can get this show, and expands the notion of value from
price to something altogether different: an experience.

Do all companies foster this same sense of inclusion? What
if, the week after your Dell arrived, you received an automatically
generated voicemail from Michael Dell asking you if you love your
computer and soliciting your feedback? Even better if it said, "Here
is my e-mail address. Send me a personal note." That would foster
intimacy and a connection. Or how about if you spent $750 on a
pair of Christian Louboutin shoes and received more than the plea-
sure of spotting other members of the red-soled shoe club? What if a
saleswoman called you the following week to find out how the shoes
were fitting, how you're doing in them, and seeing if you needed
some Band-Aids? You'd never buy Jimmy Choo again.

GRANT ALL-ACCESS PASSES.

The leadership layer of most not-for-profits is remarkably acces-
sible. In many instances you can call a not-for-profit, ask to speak
to the head of the group, and that individual will answer the phone.
And if she's not there, she'll actually call or e-mail you back. This
happens not because not-for-profit CEOs are more outgoing than

corporate types or because we have so much time on our hands. Rather, it's because we grasp the value of accessibility. We know how much difference it can make to talk with the person in charge rather than with the receptionist. We know how much donors appreciate it when the CEO or CFO or a celebrity associated with their group communicates with them. Such leaders see outsiders and stake-holders not as nuisances but as potential— or existing—partners, as people who are worthy of their time and our energy. The ROI (return on investment) here is human contact, putting a face and a voice on an often faceless entity.

Of course, the chairman and CEO of McDonald's can't spend his days talking to everyone who buys a hamburger. But perhaps he could make himself available during certain office hours. Or perhaps the company's investor-relations group could organize a live online chat or a teleconference, akin to the ones it'll hold with stock analysts, so that customers and noninstitutional investors can interact with him. Why not make the chief food technologist of the company available to engage in online forums about making better McChicken sandwiches?

When executives become too important to communicate with customers, the company loses the opportunity to give back something valuable to those customers. For example, the Acumen Fund is a well-regarded not-for-profit that funds enterprise and micro-finance projects in the developing world. Recently it received a whopping seven hundred applications from college students for the summer internship program but was only able to accept ten. The organization recognized that this pool of seven hundred applicants contained a wealth of enthusiasm, goodwill, and interest—they were potential employees as well as potential ambassadors and do-nors. How not to waste that resource? It arranged a conference call for all the rejected intern applicants. These young people didn't get the internship that they had wanted, but they got a chance to inter-act with Acumen Fund associates. It was a unique opportunity to pick the team members' brains. And it was an experience, small and low-cost but significant, that they would not soon forget.

I use that Acumen Fund example to show how simple it can be to create access as well as to diversify your events calendar away from the big gala fund-raiser. Events are a cornerstone of the not-for-profit strategy—not-for-profits invite donors to all types of events, from workshops to conferences to dances to athletic contests. These events facilitate interactions among donors, staffers, volunteers, and others. They give us an opportunity to bask in the prestige of our celebrity spokespeople. They are chances to rally enthusiasm and ramp up the excitement. And while not-for-profits mostly use these events to raise funds, we also recognize the value of providing donors with opportunities to celebrate the group's achieved goals, to learn more about the group's strategy and still-unreached goals, and to participate in face-to-face conversations among the various stakeholders.

More exciting than an invitation to an event is an invitation to travel to the field with a not-for-profit organization. Recently, charity: water took a small group of fathers and their young daughters to Africa for a chance to see one of the sustainable water wells being built. You can imagine the sense of kinship that overtook the twelve-year-old girls, whose families had donated a significant amount to the organization. Could they have spent spring vacation in Palm Beach? Sure. Instead these families helped dig wells that would deliver clean water to entire villages. They met people affected by the work of charity: water. And the trip allowed the donors and their enthusiastic youthful daughters to form a deep connection, most likely securing their club membership for next year.

Whenever I think about access—which is one of the best, most effective ways that not-for-profits look out for their donors and one of the best, most effective ways that for-profits can reward their customers—the movie *Willy Wonka & the Chocolate Factory* pops into my head. ("Violet, you're turning violet!" or "I can't swim! I can't swim!") The whole thing is outrageous, from the music to the adventures to the edible wallpaper. But the movie contains an incredibly powerful business idea: letting consumers into the actual factory to see its secrets. Look at how many chocolate bars Willy Wonka sold when he offered those golden tickets! Your organization

and mine certainly don't have that kind of mystique, but the moral of the story is still the same: people prefer to be on the inside, rather than on the outside looking in. And in today's business climate, if you have a chance to turn them into "insiders"—into brand ambassadors, into lifetime loyalists—you'd better take it.

ELEVEN QUESTIONS TO GET YOU STARTED:
Do More for Customers

Taking off my not-for-profit partner hat for a few minutes, and instead just sitting there at the headquarters of the ginormous company imagining myself as an average customer, I felt dirty. I felt like a chump. These oompa loompas were not friendly creatures who thought of me, the customer, as anything more than their next sales figure.

Seeing your customer as the enemy isn't just impractical, it's kinda weird, no? Customers are more than just people to "acquire"— they're the people who are going to drink your orange juice to grow strong, drive your car to the hospital to meet a baby grandchild, or use a loan from your bank to help pay for their first home.

Not-for-profits see our customers as our allies. How do you see your customers?

1. Is your brand nice or important to your customer? (Hint: There is a right answer to this one.)

2. When someone buys your product or service, what is she getting? Answer the question using three words, not a description of the product itself. What value does the consumer buy from you?

3. Why do your customers pick yours over other brands or other purchases that they could make for the same money?

4. Do you ever give away freebies? Are they something people actually want, or are they the cheapest item you could make with your logo on it?

5. Do you ever aggregate consumers? Do you ever give a "pass it on" coupon or a "thousandth customer served" reward?

6. Do you have any relationship with your customer after the sale? Or do you breathe a sigh of relief when the credit card goes through and the signature matches the one on the card?

7. Where do you operate? Literally write down the towns, cities, and states where you employ people. Now look at your consumer data. See anything? If not, ask yourself why your neighbors (and perhaps employees) are buying somebody else's products!

8. Can you Willy-Wonka your factory or headquarters? Have you ever considered welcoming clients or patrons to your home turf for an insider's view?

9. Given the age, gender, socioeconomic background, cultural preferences, and political leanings of your customer, what social, medical, economic, or other problems would be of primary concern to him or her? Which one resonates most on an emotional level?

10. Given the products and services your company produces as well as its corporate culture, which of these problems does it make the most sense to address? Is there a particular cause that seems a better fit for your industry, your approach to business, and your organizational norms?

11. Do you offer special access to customers to encourage their loyalty? A newsletter? Advance sales? Discounted rates? Do you treat your customers like you actually care about them?

6

DO MORE WITH YOUR BOARD

LATELY, CORPORATE BOARDS OF directors haven't won many popularity contests. In recent years, as shareholders read stories of corporate malfeasance and watched their 401(k)s shrivel, as they saw news of big salaries and bigger bonuses and sat helpless as their life savings evaporated, some of the blame rightly fell on boards. Consumer watchdog groups and politicians have accused them of shirking their governance responsibilities. They were said to be too cozy with CEOs and were lambasted for functioning more as rubber stamps than as savvy and objective advisers. It seems there might be a little room for improvement.

Let me just say flat out that not-for-profit boards are not perfect. In fact, some not-for-profit boards are more like friendly knitting circles than real guardians of good governance. I know of one not-for-profit board that meets annually for an hour; the members listen to the CEO give a boring, canned speech while they nibble on nice food. Some organizations appoint members for name value alone

or do the I'll-serve-on-your-board-if-you'll-serve-on-mine dance. Many organizations operate on a mercenary model; if a donor is generous enough, and may again be generous in the future, he or she will get a seat. Most groups are willing to live with the "law of thirds" when it comes to our boards: one-third are dead weight, one-third are sort of engaged, and one-third are truly committed.

Legally, not-for-profit and for-profit boards are quite similar. Both require a "duty of care" and a "duty of loyalty" to the organization. Simply, this means that, by law, board members are supposed to have the best interests of the corporation at heart. They must do more than just supervise; they are legally responsible for the entity's fiscal health and financial integrity. On the program or product side, board members must review and make recommendations on the big issues facing the organization.

So why, given the similarities between the two, would I still choose a not-for-profit board over a for-profit one nine times out of ten? Because one of the great differences that I've found between them is the philosophy. In the for-profit world, board members are motivated by desire for prestige, desire for status, and sense of obligation. People aspire to retire and spend their final days fishing, golfing, and flitting around the country to serve on corporate boards. In my world, however, board members are the owners of the enterprise. They're an essential part of the team.

I don't believe I'm being cynical when I assert that most for-profit company directors are motivated to serve by the cachet, the perks, the networking possibilities, some quid pro quo (perhaps the CEO or another board member did them a favor, and they're returning it by agreeing to join the board), and/or the money. A directorship is something of a trophy placed on the mantle, a sign of accomplishment above and beyond being a top executive. Often board members have no vested interest in helping a company succeed beyond the financial—and outside directors often own only minimal stakes in the company. They're not necessarily passionate about its products or services. Often they have no strong links to the company and little awareness of its culture or history.

At most not-for-profits, board members are usually motivated by their passion for the specific cause. They generally don't have much to gain—and they know we're going to keep asking them for their money, their contacts, and their in-kind contributions. They are not disinterested observers, because we won't let them be. Even if they're serving on the board as a favor to a friend, we make sure that they know it is a big favor. Our purpose becomes important to them. Our work becomes their work. If your for-profit board members behaved more like not-for-profit board members, it would greatly affect your company's culture and behavior and perhaps lead to different results. And isn't that really what you want from a board member—to have a direct impact on your company, rather than just a fancy name on your letterhead? In this chapter, I'll explore what it takes to make that happen.

ADJUST YOUR SELECTION CRITERIA.

The problems start when you're looking for board members. At worst, corporations seek board members with the biggest names, the people who will impress shareholders, or the CEO's golf buddies. The fancy firm you've hired to find good candidates wants to impress you with the stature of their list. The pool of candidates is often ridiculously, incestuously small. Take a quick flip through a pile of Fortune 500 annual reports. You'll see a lot of retirees—former this and ex that. This is the corporate board as career pasture. CEOs tout their board members' vast past experience, but how about current network? Are they connected to the latest trends in technology—or do they still refer to the Internet as the World Wide Web? Why do so few boards in the for-profit world have what many not-for-profits seek—people who are younger, more innovative, more primed for networking, hungrier?

As you peruse the group photos of corporate boards, you'll also notice the tokenism and how the same faces repeatedly crop up to fill the de rigueur woman and minority slots. At a conference two years

ago I heard Laura d'Andrea Tyson, the Clinton administration official who now teaches at UC–Berkeley's Haas School of Business, speak about the "male and pale" syndrome that afflicts corporate boards. Tyson, who sits on the boards of Morgan Stanley, AT&T, and Eastman Kodak, is right. According to an article in *Fortune*, women occupy only one out of every six company directorships. Being that women make up half the population, that seems a bit disproportionate, no? Even companies that talk about diversity as a priority don't apply that principle to their corporate board membership. Chrysler has an explicit corporate diversity policy, but its board is lagging. Some industry observers have described its board as "a male frat party at the Vatican" and "a white polar bear in an igloo." To Tyson's denotation of male and pale, I'd also add stale. Most of these board members are old!

The question is, how does this happen? One reason is basic human nature. We tend to gravitate to people who are like us, not just in race and age but in so many other ways, from schooling to career to club affiliations. Another reason is the homogeneity of the upper echelons of the corporate world—big companies want board members with extensive big-company experience and accomplishment, and these people tend to be older white males. To their credit, some companies are making a more active effort to select more diverse boards, just as corporate America is striving for more diverse management, but the progress is slow, as some still need to be convinced that it's a valuable priority.

It's not that I don't like old white guys; it's that I don't think any kind of homogeneity is helpful. If the board is entirely young black women or middle-aged Greenwich Connecticuters or any other like-minded group, then the board will be limited in its ability to help the organization question, stretch, learn, grow, and succeed.

There will always be some cronyism in board selection. It happens all the time in the not-for-profit world too. Of course we pull in people we know. Of course we try to recruit our friends. But ultimately my organization isn't going to be helped by a board member who looks just like me. I've already got the downtown New York

working-mom thing covered. I need people who can work other circles. A board is really a collection of individuals, and each needs to pull their own weight. As Peter Wilderotter, the head of the Christopher and Dana Reeve Foundation, likes to say, "It's only a board when you bring them together. Most of the time you're working with these people as individuals, so you need each of them to bring something to the table."

I've always been highly conscious of the need to bring in board members with complementary skills. If my organization has fifteen board members who all are good at raising money from a single source and none has any expertise in strategic development, that won't do us much good. If we're heavy on board members who can provide advice on communication, of course we avoid bringing in a new board member with the same expertise.

Kate Roberts, the head of YouthAIDS, recently shared with me that she was looking for a board member at a senior level in the media or advertising world. She's working on the launch of an important new initiative and hopes to find someone who can help direct the strategy, tone, and execution of a multimedia campaign. As we spoke, it occurred to me that if she hadn't said the words "board member," we could have been talking about a typical staff opening, about filling a hole and meeting a skill need on the team. Not-for-profit board members are like senior staff who won't be in the office every day or even every week and will never get a paycheck from the organization.

ENCOURAGE A SERVICE MIND-SET.

Corporate boards tend to have an ownership mentality. Whether they actually are partial owners through the stock they hold or simply act as if they are owners because they have exalted director status, they are much more likely to ask what others can do for the company than to ask what they themselves can do. This isn't just a question of semantics. Owners are privileged. They stand (or more often just sit) on high. They give orders.

You'll rarely find that entitlement mentality on not-for-profit boards. In most instances they recognize that they serve for the good of the organization and not the other way around. For example, one of my most powerful board members at Dress for Success was a woman named Marge Magner. At the time, she was the head of Citibank—and the most senior woman in banking in the world. Citi was a sponsor and friend of the organization, but we had the chance to work with two other rivals, Chase and Bank of America, on high-profile partnerships. Although Marge was a real Citi champion, she blessed the new partnerships and wished us every success promoting the heck out of those programs because she knew it was the best thing for Dress for Success. That is the kind of selfless commitment we expect (and cherish) in not-for-profit board members.

Big companies could use more directors with this at-the-service-of-the-company mentality. In many not-for-profits, board members come up with highly creative solutions. They feel compelled to suggest new policies and practices, and even if their suggestions are not all adopted, they're eager and willing to serve their groups by being creative. A greater degree of passion for the company might create a greater sense of urgency. A service approach to the position might mean that instead of just supervising, they would work at fresh thinking. This mind-set might also inspire proactive problem-solving before something reaches a crisis level. And boards that feel they are there to serve the company might conduct greater oversight of the CEO, truly asking, *Is he the best person for this company right now?*

PUT YOUR TARGET MARKET ON THE BOARD.

One reason some board members may not feel deeply connected to the company they serve is that they're detached from its target market. For example, Abercrombie & Fitch, a company that sells casual clothing to teens and young adults, doesn't have a single person under the age of fifty-four on its board. Might the board be more

effective if someone who actually shopped at Abercrombie (or still had kids in that target age group) sat on that board? I think so.

I'm always astonished when I examine the background of board members of a big company and discover little connection to the target market. You'd think that a company like Procter & Gamble, whose product list is dominated by goods that either primarily target women or are most often purchased by women, would have that constituency well represented on its board of directors. But just two of its thirteen directors are female. Unilever, another consumer-products giant that makes everything from laundry detergent to frozen foods to makeup to soap, has on its eleven-strong board a lone female member. Can you imagine being the lone voice representing well over half the target market in board meetings? Mucho pressure! Wouldn't it be helpful to have more than one person in the room who can speak from personal experience—or at least has an affinity with the target market? Sure, board meetings are dominated by discussions of numbers and governance issues, but those numbers represent actual people and sales and products. Perhaps having a few people at the table from that mind-set would help push the board to think in new ways.

Perhaps because not-for-profits are driven by impact as well as by numbers, we strive to make sure our various constituencies, including the target market, are represented on the board. Feeding America—whose mission is to feed the country's hungry through a network of pantries and food banks—is a fine example. Its board is a representative mix of the companies that contribute, including executives from Walmart, Mars, and Campbell's Soup, as well as the organizations that benefit from Feeding America's work, including the leaders of food banks from Maryland, Ohio, and Texas.

New York's Robin Hood Foundation, dedicated to eradicating poverty in all its forms (see Chapter 4), is astonishingly adept at raising huge sums of money from its donors. Not surprisingly, its board of directors includes Wall Street wizards like hedge fund pioneer Paul Tudor Jones and celebrities like Gwyneth Paltrow, but even this big-name board also includes activists like Geoffrey Canada of

Harlem Children's Zone. Communities in Schools, a not-for-profit organization that helps children stay in school, is another example of a well-balanced board that includes a child services expert, school superintendents, and educators from other institutions. Additionally, Communities in Schools has a Learning Council to supplement its standard board. This secondary board, even more heavily populated with educators and experts, serves as an additional voice of reason and experience.

DON'T COMPENSATE BOARD MEMBERS.

Not-for-profit board members are rarely paid. In fact, they often are expected to "pay back" the not-for-profits that bring them on board through donations, fund-raising, and advice. Many not-for-profit boards even have explicit "give or get" policies, stating very plainly how much money a board member will need to give or go get from someone else. For example, the Human Rights Campaign is one of the largest and most powerful gay rights organizations in the country. Its "give or get" policy is $50,000. But that's nothing compared to Robin Hood's, which is rumored to be more than double that amount.

This suggestion isn't going to be popular with those "career directors," but in the not-for-profit environment we've learned that not paying board members ensures that their motivation for being on the board isn't monetary. While their reasons for accepting a position may not be completely selfless—they may like the prestige, they may want to expand their networks—they are often motivated by their belief in the group's purpose or by the challenge with which the group presents them. My friend Jim Berrien, the former president of *Forbes,* was on the board of the National Eating Disorders Association (NEDA) for a while because he was the father of a daughter facing these issues. He genuinely cared about stemming anorexia and bulimia and wanted to help the organization grow. He even wrote an autobiographical piece for *Newsweek* about his per-

sonal learning curve as a father surprised by his daughter's sudden weight loss and emotional struggle. So Jim had extremely personal reasons for being part of that NEDA board of directors. He was also on my board at Dress for Success. Why? Because as the president of *Forbes*, he instituted a *Forbes* conference on women, created the Trailblazer Award for women, and cared about the progress of women in the workplace—even at those entry levels. So his motivation for joining the Dress for Success board was a commitment to the purpose of our organization but also part of his work priorities.

How do you figure out someone's motivations for joining a board? You can ask them but, better yet, make them actually spend some time in your store. Make sure they use your product. Have they ever purchased something from your website? Are they in your records as a subscriber? If they have no connection to your company, product, or service, why do they want to be on your board? And more important, why do you want them?

CREATE EXPLICIT GUIDELINES FOR BOARD MEMBERS.

Over the last few years, as scandal after corporate scandal has hit the business pages in both hemispheres, millions of people around the world have been asking themselves this question: What exactly does a board member do? A good board—be it for-profit or not—will spell out the responsibilities and expectations of board membership. The bylaws that govern a board must make explicit things like term length and the process of selection/termination. A really smart organization will create an additional document that spells out the board members' extralegal job. For example, at Do Something, board members are required to serve on at least one board committee. They must attend our annual event in person. And of course, we have a "give or get" policy to drive board dollars.

The real genius of the Robin Hood Foundation isn't who is on the board but how the board operates: it is hands on, committed, and innovative in its approach. The board establishes metrics

for effectiveness and holds "grantees" (those who receive foundation monies) accountable for their performance. A lot of for-profit boards don't like getting into metrics and accountability. Not only does it take a lot of work to orchestrate, but they have to make difficult decisions that can upset stakeholders. Boards rarely tell the CEO that a major supplier isn't meeting the company's criteria for partnership or that they should no longer work with a customer whose policies violate the company's values.

The Robin Hood board has a system in place that compares the relative return of any two grants. They measure how a given grantee has used the money to increase young adult earnings for poor people, and their formula helps them compare the performance of one grantee versus another. In this way, they make sure they don't continue funding mediocre or poor performers and their money goes to groups that are doing the most good. Every year, about 10 percent of grantees lose their funding based on this performance measure. No doubt it's tough for the board to enforce this measurement and tell people no, but all boards should be willing and able to do it. Being part of this board means that you will personally weigh in on grant decisions.

MEET IN THE FIELD.

The Robin Hood Foundation board's four annual meetings are not held in law offices or foundation headquarters. Instead, board members travel to New York City locations where they're funding programs, meeting in a school cafeteria or the computer room of a literacy organization they've funded.

No matter how wonderful the board members, no matter how successful the company, a board meeting can still "suck." It can be too long. It can be overrun by one domineering member. It can have too much review and not enough question time. It can be too big. It can be too small, rendering it quorumless and pointless. It can be too disorganized or too structured. There are so many ways a board meeting can go wrong.

It's impossible for anyone to guarantee a board meeting that is scintillating, well attended, productive, and all-around great. But I do have one piece of advice from the not-for-profit sector that can help: meet in the field. Most of the people on your board have probably already met their lifetime quotas for meetings in wood-paneled conference rooms with gourmet cookies.

Endeavor is an organization that funds high-impact entrepreneurs in impoverished markets. Founder and CEO Linda Rottenberg insists that the board meet in the field. As part of its effort to reduce global poverty by investing in various countries throughout the developing world, Endeavor takes its board members to visit the portfolio companies and meet these entrepreneurs—even in remote parts of Africa. These trips and personal experiences provide perspective and a more comprehensive understanding of the portfolio companies than is available from spreadsheets and pretty photos.

In August 2006, for the first anniversary of Hurricanes Katrina and Rita, KaBOOM! brought its board members to New Orleans to meet, to help lead a playground build, and to witness the devastation that inspired Operation Playground, KaBOOM!'s campaign to bring play back to the Gulf Coast after the storms.

Our best-attended Dress for Success board meetings were always at the shop itself.

Why not hold your Walmart board meeting in the employee coffee room of a nearby store? Or host a Starbucks board meeting at a local Starbucks after hours?

DON'T PUT THE CEO ON THE BOARD.

I don't sit on the board of Do Something. When I first took the job here, they offered me the role of CEO and board president. And because that was offered to me, I nearly didn't take either. I believe that an organization that would hand over both roles to one person—especially one outside person—isn't taking its governance seriously. Instead, I politely turned down the president role and ac-

cepted the CEO spot. To this day, I'm not a member of the board. Do I attend board meetings? Of course. Do I do most of the speaking? (If you've not seen me in meetings, you can safely just nod yes to that last question.) Do I help create the agenda? Absolutely. But I don't have a vote.

It's a policy shared by, not all, but many other heads of not-for-profits. For one thing, we recognize the value of a system of checks and balances and especially the value of having outside governance that can act truly independently and without our meddling. For another, if I'm confident that the individuals on my board of directors are sincerely serving for the good of the organization, why should I need a vote? Am I that much of a control freak? The CEO can be in the room and even play a vital role in the meeting without having a vote.

Boards that operate independently of the CEO can be more effective. Board independence sends the message that members' opinions truly matter, so they may be more willing to express their views when they know the CEO isn't on the board. Organizations thrive when a diversity of opinions and an independent-minded board can point out problems or opportunities that the executive branch might miss. CEO-free boards are in a good position to provide this kind of true governance—they possess the mandate to point out financial irregularities and identify ethics violations. They have the autonomy to question me and my decisions fearlessly. And I'm keenly aware of that power.

This structure is even more vital in founder-led companies. At Dress for Success I was never on the board of directors. In fact, one of my favorite board meetings involved hot debate over a policy I held dear: noncompetition. I felt that Dress for Success should not enter markets where something similar already existed. But we had received numerous applications from Chicago and Washington, D.C., two markets where organizations similar to Dress for Success had existed for years. After extensive, intensive debate, the board voted to disagree with me, abandon the noncompetition policy, and grant a franchise start-up license to an applicant in Chicago.

I was sad to lose the debate, but that night I celebrated with a glass of champagne. The day the board of directors overruled the founder was a day Dress for Success achieved a certain measure of maturity. It wasn't a club with a crazy woman as the omnipotent head but a vibrant institution capable of debate, decision, and dissent. And of overruling that crazy woman.

ENCOURAGE THE BOARD TO COMMUNICATE DIRECTLY WITH STAFF.

Good board members are like a human how-to manual: wise men and women who have seen and done it all, and whom you can consult as needed. They know the mistakes people often make when launching growth strategies; they know the industry backward and forward; they have skills that range from finance to marketing to technology. What if they were to share this knowledge with the appropriate employees? What if they were to work side by side with your biz dev guy on a key project to accomplish an important objective? Companies frequently hire expensive outside consultants who may not be privy to the knowledge or inner workings of a company that a board member has access to.

Why hire an expensive consultant when you can accrue wonderful help for free? Peter D'Amelio was the COO of The Cheesecake Factory. Based on how much cheesecake that restaurant produces on a daily basis, it is fair to assume that Peter is a busy man. But busy people are willing—even eager—to lend time and expertise to serve on a not-for-profit board where they can have an impact. For that reason Peter (after sitting next to KaBOOM! founder Darell Hammond on an airplane) joined the KaBOOM! board in 2000, bringing his operational expertise.

At the time, KaBOOM! was a young organization in need of advice. Building playgrounds across the country involves a lot of moving pieces, insurance, people, and so on. Alongside the staff, Peter helped draft the first set of policies and procedures. These policies

live on today and exist only because he pushed the organization to document its work flow, to examine how various departments interact, and to constantly stay in check with its guiding standards. The Cheesecake Factory may not match KaBOOM!'s purpose—one promotes eating while the other facilitates childhood play—but Peter's operational experience and willingness to spend time with the staff led to the creation of a useful map guiding its work flow.

If you were to ask a director of General Motors or IBM how many different employees he's talked to or worked with in the past year on a meaningful project, his answer would probably be one or two (if that). Besides the CEO, he may have had conversations with the CFO about a key financial issue, or he may have interacted with the human resources chief about a succession plan, but that's about it. The separation of directors and employees is due, in part, to the CEO's reluctance to integrate the two groups. I've heard more than one CEO express his fear that if his people had access to board members, all they'd do is complain about everything from their compensation to the CEO's shortcomings to the lack of amenities in the third-floor bathroom. And yes, it would be counterproductive for board members to be bombarded with some of these issues. But this kind of transparency and knowledge might also lead to a more informed and therefore useful board.

Not-for-profit boards usually have at least twice as many members as corporate boards—according to BoardSource, the average not-for-profit board has seventeen members. My boards usually have around twenty. Museum boards have as many as fifty! To keep all these people involved and informed, not-for-profits encourage interactions between board members and staff. At Do Something my CTO and CMO and even some junior staff talk to our board as much as, if not more than, I do. In some instances the interactions between people are formalized; they serve on committees addressing issues like marketing or technology. In other instances the interactions are informal—staff people call board members for advice in the board member's area of expertise. At some not-for-profits a staffer is designated as the coordinator of board-staff relationships.

Planned Parenthood, for instance, has established an entire position specifically designed to facilitate the flow of communication between board members and staffers.

Why is this interaction important for companies? First, it gives key employees access to both expertise and wisdom that they may have difficulty finding anywhere else. A given board member may be a world-class expert in sales, marketing, finance, or one hundred other subjects; he knows the best practices in a given area. This same board member may also be an industry veteran, someone who has seen and done it all, and so can provide sage counsel to those with less experience. And best of all in tough economic times, his advice is free. Why deny employees access to this incredibly valuable resource? Someone or some policy has to regulate these relationships, but that's more a question of details and execution than of philosophy.

Second, integrating staff and board members is a great way to keep the board informed and involved. I would bet that in any major company a sizable percentage of the directors would like to be more engaged in the problems and opportunities confronting the company, but they feel like they don't know enough and that their help isn't really needed. Establishing regular relationships between board members and employees would demonstrate that their knowledge is valued, and it would also keep them up to date about what is happening in key corporate areas.

REQUIRE BOARD MEMBERS TO LOVE YOUR PURPOSE.

Do all the board members of Sprint use that cell service? Do the board members of Sears actually shop there for holiday gifts? Do the board members of Harley-Davidson ride Harleys—or at least love people who do?

Good not-for-profit board members become zealots for the brand. They love to carry the tote bag, talk about the organization, and most important, recruit other people to be involved. They do

so because they love our products or services. At Dress for Success we required the board members to dress clients at least twice a year. At KaBOOM! the board members must participate in at least one build a year. And at Teach For America the board members must visit a classroom at least once each school year.

At not-for-profits, many members are recruited based on their passion for the cause. Thus they arrive ready, willing, and able to help their organization in many different ways. They don't want to be passive overseers; they want to be involved. Curing cancer and cleaning up the environment are easier causes to be passionate about than selling insurance or laundry detergent, but for-profit companies could still make an effort to recruit more board members that have an inherent concern about them. Perhaps the members love the company's products or services. Maybe they admire the company's vision and values. Perhaps they once worked for the company and still have strong ties to it. Maybe they see the company as having the potential to go from good to great, and they want to be part of that journey. Such individuals are infinitely more likely to contribute above and beyond the norm—and keeping them connected to the underlying cause helps keep them motivated and involved.

Reid Hoffman, the founder and CEO of LinkedIn, is a fantastic example of someone who does this. As a board member of Kiva, the online microfinance not-for-profit, Hoffman has actively recruited people not just to be board members and partners but also to make loans—because he is effusive about the power of microfinance and, specifically, Kiva. What makes him a good board member is his brilliance and connections. What makes him a great board member is his love of the product.

If board members have anything in abundance, it's connections. Are your board members acting as ambassadors for the company? If not, why not? They know a lot of influential people, and they're often good at identifying advantageous matches. Corporations tend not to partner enough, and when they do, they frequently partner with the most obvious parties. Board members could help them expand their universe of relationships, by providing the introductions

to other individuals and groups and also by suggesting good partnerships. Not-for-profits' board members help organizations connect with a wide variety of people—sponsors for events, suppliers, donors, advisers, prospective employees, and possible partners—and they are much better equipped to be salespeople if they actually know the product. If they are not using their assets to help the company, I suspect it's because they don't care about it. Get them to interact with your product, your service, and your customer, and they will want to help the company thrive.

ELEVEN QUESTIONS TO GET YOU STARTED:
Do More with Your Board

How much do for-profit boards really add to their companies? If you talk to most corporate executives—and can get them to speak in all candor—they'll answer, "Not much." In many cases, corporate execs don't want them to add anything; they just want them to rubber-stamp decisions and stay out of the way. Even in the post-Sarbanes-Oxley era, boards may well serve a purpose, but it's still a limited one. Providing financial oversight is appreciated—not to mention legally required—but it's really not sufficient. If you look at the directors of any Fortune 100 company, you'll find a lot of underutilized knowledge and skill. We don't have room in the not-for-profit world for that kind of waste. If you have knowledge and skill, we're going to milk it. For-profits have every reason to do the same.

The thing that I keep learning and relearning is that my board and the people on it are only as good as I make them. If they're not being utilized, it's my fault for not tapping them. If they're not interacting with the brand, it's because I'm not creating opportunities for them to do so. And if they're the wrong people—or the wrong

mix of people—it's my fault for not composing a good and balanced board.

Here's the good news. Making the most of your board is something totally within your control. It's completely realistic to envision a point in the near future when someone asks you what your board really adds to your company, and you say, "How much time have you got? I don't even know where to begin."

Here are eleven questions to help you get started:

1. Where do you have board meetings? Are you in a nondescript office? Or are you "in the field," near your product or service?

2. Plot a board meeting on a graph chart. Who talks? What are the key topics? Are you diversified?

3. Do you have explicit board membership guidelines? Are they enforced? Who is responsible for enforcing them?

4. Is your CEO on the board? Has your board ever disagreed or outvoted the CEO? Was that viewed as a sign of independence or animosity?

5. Are your board members compensated? If you stopped compensating them, would they still serve?

6. Why are these people on your board? What interests them? Why are they serving your company and not your competition, or a bigger flashier board?

7. When was the last time each board member used or interacted with your product or service?

8. How diverse is your board? Not just by age, race, and gender but also by experience set.

9. Do your board members talk about the company? Is your company in their bio? Is your product or service proudly displayed in their home? Have they sent other people and partnerships your way?

10. Do your board members communicate with your team? Chart those relationships on paper. Make those connections explicit in your mind. Is it just the same few people?

11. Bottom line: Do you think of your board as a real asset, a benign entity, or a hindrance?

7

DO MORE WITH YOUR STAFF

AS I LOOKED AROUND the ginormous company's conference room at these panicked unhappy people, I saw the need for chocolate, Advil, and maybe a good shrink. These were the employees of *Dilbert* and *Cathy* and *The Office*: stressed out and fearful. I was beginning to think that, like most clichés, this walking stereotype exists for a very good reason: it's true.

Figuring out how to use your staff efficiently is a challenge. Hiring, promoting, and firing have become such complex responsibilities that corporations have created reams of rules and regulations to govern the processes and entire human resource departments to enforce them. Before you can hire people, you must consider the job specs; factor in diversity issues; figure if the applicants are who they say they are (since references are hard to come by in these litigious times); and determine if they will mesh with the culture. To fire them, you have to build your case and create a treatise documenting your reasons, while trying to predict what lawsuit you might have to

defend. To promote people, you have to consider so many criteria—expertise, experience, seniority, and so on—that it makes your head dance the tango. Oh, and did I mention the forms? You have to fill out forms. Lots and lots of forms.

Do you hate the complexity of hiring, promoting, and firing at your company? Are you losing high-performing people after a year or two? Are there people who have "fallen up" the corporate ladder mostly because they continued to show up and not because they're particularly talented or useful?

Not-for-profits struggle with the same issues, but we have some secrets. They don't solve all the problems inherent in human resources, but great not-for-profits have been able to amplify the contributions of top talent by maximizing one guiding principle: passion. To us, passion almost always trumps expertise and experience. There's nothing wrong with experience and expertise, but as not-for-profits have learned, there's a lot more right with passion.

Who is a passionate employee? The one who keeps a meeting going because she refuses to accept the good-but-not-great idea that has achieved consensus; the one who risks irritating others because he's convinced, absolutely convinced, that unless they work harder to find the right solution, the project will fail; the one who is so committed to finding that idea that she keeps a notepad next to her bed so she can jot down ideas if they occur to her in the middle of the night; the one who will skip meals and break dinner dates if he thinks he's close to figuring out that next new thing.

Not-for-profits naturally attract a lot of idealistic individuals, people who believe in a given cause and are working for principles rather than profit. But not all of them are passionate about it. They may be nice people who believe in the right things, but they aren't driven. Out of necessity, not-for-profits have had to separate the passionless from the passionate. We hire and promote the latter. When we have to let people go, the first on the chopping block are the ones who don't use their Facebook status updates to promote the brand.

Seriously. Is your job penetrating your conscious and taking over your personal life? If so, you're the kind of employee we love.

We're not always right in our decisions—we've made "bad hires" too—but we've developed tactics that usually help us identify those who are deeply dedicated to the work.

Wait a second, you might be thinking. What about the veteran who knows the ropes? What about the employee with a high skill level? Aren't these attributes more valuable and promotable than passion?

If I had to choose between a passionless Ivy League grad with ten years of experience and great skills and a high-school dropout with less experience and skills but an abundance of enthusiasm, I'd take David over Goliath every time.

Experience is overrated. Somebody else trained that person. He could be stuck in his old ways. And expertise can be taught. My husband was a consultant for years and likes to say that he can learn almost any business in about a week of intense study. (Of course, there are exceptions. I wouldn't want him operating on my brain after only a week of study.) In general, experience and expertise are overrated.

Passion, however, is invaluable. If passionate people don't have the experience to know something, they make it their business to find it out. If they require an expert skill to do a job well, they acquire it. They're motivated to deliver outstanding work. Passion catalyzes superior performance.

Here's an example of how passion motivates people to learn what they need to know to do a good job. This nice young guy named George once interviewed for a public relations job at Do Something. He didn't know much about media, but in his interview he came off as a true believer. He had clearly spent a lot of time trolling our website. He asked questions that demonstrated a keen appreciation of our purpose, brand, and target market. In his free time he was volunteering at his old high school, which showed a genuine commitment to young people.

Plus, George was a long-distance runner in college. Wall Street likes to hire lacrosse and football players. I like to hire long-distance runners and rowers. These people run or row in a straight line, for

hours—and sometimes in the dark. They aren't racing necessarily against each other, but against themselves, trying to surpass their last personal best. Google-Image the word *diligence,* and you should find pictures of rowers with the sun rising behind them, steam coming off the water in winter, and tired bags under their eyes. Both sports require dedication and perseverance to achieve goals, and yet the rewards are not immediate and often occur out of the spotlight. When is the last time a rower or a long-distance runner was featured in a Nike ad or paraded around town with a supermodel girlfriend? Unfortunately, there is little glory in running a four-minute mile . . . unless you happen to apply for a job in my employment.

So we hired George. Actually, I invented a job for him. Not in public relations—George had never watched *Access Hollywood* and couldn't name a single JLo song or film. I figured his knack for perseverance might make him a good fund-raiser, so we tried him at corporate cause marketing. He turned out to be a lousy salesperson. He had a high IQ, but he wasn't a relationship-driven type of guy. He didn't suffer fools easily.

Did we fire him? I thought about it. I would have been justified—we really didn't have a spot for his limited experience and expertise. But I loved his passion. He was the first person to work every morning and the last to turn off the lights at the end of the day. He sent me ideas by text message on Saturday nights. And he even pulled his younger sister into the office to intern during school breaks. So we moved him again, this time to our technology group.

George didn't have much tech experience. Actually, he didn't have any tech experience and never imagined himself in a tech job. (Remember, he came in applying for the PR position.) But he bought one of the "Dummies" books and taught himself MySQL and HTML. He read everything he could find in book format and online to learn about search optimization. And he was the first person to volunteer to participate in any brainstorm with another department or crisis-management task force; he was a killer team player.

When our CTO was hired away by the *New York Post*, George wanted the job. Instead, I brought in a new CTO, someone with a

tremendous amount of experience, and we paid him a commensu-
rately high salary because of that experience. George worked under
him, and I thought it would be a great opportunity for him to absorb
information and ideas from this more senior guy.

The new CTO, however, was awful. He considered himself su-
perior stock and wouldn't listen to other people. He was set in his
ways, insisting that we use a different system to code the site—and
that he should write this code in the seclusion of his home, instead
of in the office. He was so expert that he was ill suited to function-
ing as a part of a team, believing his track record entitled him to a
certain degree of autonomy.

Worst of all, he went about his job like a bureaucratic function-
ary. He knew his stuff, but he didn't bring any charisma or character
to it. He didn't inspire or motivate others. He had no interest in
mentoring the incredibly hungry aforementioned George. And he
was perfectly pleased settling for a good solution instead of pursu-
ing of a great one. His attitude? He thought we should be grateful
that he was willing to grace us with his presence. Our response? We
canned him.

But I was still reluctant to name George as CTO. Instead I cre-
ated a title for him, director of technology, and held out the plum of
him being named CTO if he could grow into the job. He responded
as a long-distance runner should, wanting to beat his previous time
for the course. He didn't just work hard—he worked with imagina-
tion and inspiration. Less than a year after landing the job, he flipped
our entire website—including the content management system, ar-
chitecture, and user interface. The works. As a result of George's
leadership, we won a 2009 Webby Award, the tech world's equivalent
of an Oscar. And it wasn't in the not-for-profit category. We smacked
down MTV and Marvel comics for the best site for youth. George
now has the title of CTO, and while he still runs miles every day, he
walks with a bit of a well-earned swagger.

Not-for-profits recognize that we can't afford to lose good people
like George. Terminating passionate people is wasteful. Moreover,
George's story is no secret in our office, which incentivizes others

to follow his example: if they work hard and dedicate themselves to our purpose, I'll find a way to use them. Passionate people always have a place in my office.

Are people at General Motors and AT&T hired or promoted because of their energy and enthusiasm? Are skilled, senior people in big companies ever fired because they lack enthusiasm? Does one employee bleed the corporate colors, while another, more experienced employee, who exhibits less vigor, snags the promotion? For-profit companies hire, fire, and promote based on a clear set of criteria that has been in place for many years. Some of those criteria include:

"He's an HBS man."

"She worked for Jack Welch for years."

"He sold his first company for millions."

Gee, with nice objective criteria like these, why inject a messy intangible like passion into the hiring, firing, and promotion processes? But those past performance measures and fancy credentials don't necessarily dictate how someone will actually behave. And what you want—what you should want—is dedication, diligence, and enthusiasm. I'm not suggesting you drop pedigree as a criterion. I'm suggesting you add passion as a crucial prerequisite. These things are not mutually exclusive. Your company deserves someone experienced *and* enthusiastic.

ENSURE THAT HIGH PERFORMERS RISE TO THE TOP AND LOW PERFORMERS EXIT.

Companies have been accused of having transactional cultures, focusing their time and attention mainly on selling the most product at the least cost. Even when leadership espouses higher-level values, everyone knows that the company is all about profit. Leaders may be sincere when they call for greater openness and honesty, but in reality these values get pushed to the side in the recruitment and rewards processes.

Organizations that want to move away from being purely transactional cultures should make passion for the work a key criterion. Notice I didn't say passion for the *cause*. I truly mean passion for the work—for putting in long hours, for double-checking documents so they are typo-free, for calling on personal friends and contacts. A company that makes cardboard boxes can emulate this principle. When individuals who are hardworking, enthusiastic, and caring are hired and then appointed to key positions, other employees get the message that management is serious about those values.

Seniority-based promotions can encourage associate-level mediocrity. At most major corporations you'll find senior people who have retired in place. They climb onto the "corporate treadmill" and just keep walking. They might not go anywhere, but so long as they put one foot in front of another, they'll never fall off either. These people have no fear of being let go; they assume that their experience and expertise protects them.

In companies that reward time over talent, many younger managers punch the time clock rather than strive for excellence. In fact, they have a greater incentive to play politics and muster support for a promotion than to take risks and allow a performance to speak for itself.

At not-for-profits, we've learned that passion correlates with achievement. People know they'll be rewarded for going at a job with gusto. They understand that if they go above and beyond the call of duty, their work will be recognized.

Adam Sterling, subject of the 2007 documentary film *Darfur Now* and the founder of the Sudan Divestment Task Force, became a not-for-profit superstar solely because of his zeal and fierce determination (see Chapter 1). Fueled by pizza and college friendships, Adam mounted a campaign to persuade members of Congress to divest from Sudan. Using persistence and powerful words, he and his college friends managed to influence congresspeople toward a divestment policy. His only asset when he began was his passion.

HIRE LEADERS WHO ARE CHIEF PASSION OFFICERS.

Good not-for-profits are meritocracies. In most of them, the leaders are the most vibrant, hardest-working people in the organization. If you were to give a lie detector test to ten heads of successful not-for-profits and ten corporate CEOs, the most telling contrast would be in their levels of genuine evangelical zeal for what they do. You don't find many cold-blooded brilliant bureaucrats heading not-for-profits. Our blood runs very hot.

The individual who plays his cards close to the vest may be a great poker player, but he isn't the type of CEO who inspires others. A stoic, coldly authoritative CEO sends the message that stoicism is the model for being promoted; if you want to get ahead, adopt this style.

Not-for-profits are generally run by people who make no secret of their dedication and enthusiasm for our particular cause. We're not afraid to speak emotionally about what we're trying to accomplish. We're also perfectly willing to speak out against powerful interests that impede our organization's efforts, using fiery rhetoric to get our points across.

Do all CEOs understand that they set the tone? If they're passionate about what they do, then others will follow suit. Obviously personalities vary, and not every CEO can be a Steve Jobs. But as a corporate leader, you can be a Chief Passion Officer in a quiet way; you can demonstrate in one-on-one conversations, in white papers, and even in e-mails that you are committed to achieving your organization's goals and that you possess tremendous faith in your team's efforts. You don't have to proclaim your passion from the rooftops, but you do have to find your particular way to proclaim it.

One of the first questions people are asked in a not-for-profit job interview is, why do you care about the company? Care. Compassion is an actual job criterion.

Greg Baldwin has been at VolunteerMatch since he helped create it more than ten years ago. The only thing he is missing is a set

of pom-poms and a short skirt. That guy's title might be CEO, but really he is the Chief Cheerleader.

The other day I had a conversation with Aaron Pereira, who founded the Canadian organization Vartana and has a zillion other good not-for-profit start-up ideas in mind. He confessed to me, "How am I ever going to find a woman I love as much as I love my work? I'm consumed by it. Isn't she going to feel like my mistress?" Not-for-profit leaders typically *live* the brand. Our vacations are work conferences. Our closest friends are the people we work with. And many times they actually end up donating money back to the organization. I spent my twenties essentially married to Dress for Success. I went two entire years without kissing anyone, and spent seven all-nighters at the office during that time. (Yes, I kept a toothbrush at the office.)

Can you imagine the impact that this kind of passion would have if it came from corporate leaders? What if your office manager really cared about what your company makes? She might count those delivery boxes and take closer note of slippage, and she might spend five minutes searching for a cheaper shipping rate. Instead of hiring mercenaries, how about making genuine passion for the company's purpose the number one criterion for employment and promotion, and lack of it a potential reason for termination?

GET LEAN.

Not-for-profits are typically short-staffed. The resulting heavy workload tends to weed out the uninspired, quickly. It's a cheap tactic, literally. But staying lean does encourage a certain level of team spirit.

The Innocence Project, according to its website, was "founded in 1992 to help prisoners who could be proven innocent through DNA testing. To date, 240 people have been found innocent including 17 who served time on death row. These people serve an average of 12 years before exoneration and release." If you asked the

determined but small team of full-time lawyers on the staff, "What's your biggest challenge?" you might think they'd mention battling the court system, coping with client depression, or resisting political pressure. In fact, they'll say it's keeping up with the amount of work they have. The caseload outpaces the number of positions they can afford. It's a lean, mean team.

I would ask corporate leaders (at least the ones who are passionate about their work) to think about what their organizations would be like if they downsized their workforces by eliminating the bored, the uninspired, and the uncommitted. How might that impact morale? How might that affect productivity? What if the employees were aware that in the next downsizing, the individuals most vulnerable would be those who are just going through the motions, that their seniority no longer protects them?

Constant overwork doesn't help morale either—unless people love what they do. Ever notice that happy people don't complain about being overworked? They talk about being busy. I suspect your office can afford to lose the "overworked."

In many for-profit organizations, the rule persists, "Last one hired, first one fired." Some corporations are rumored to favor getting rid of high-salaried executives, replacing them with younger, lower-salaried ones. Neither option strikes me as beneficial. Passion for a job is not age-dependent. Salary, too, has no impact on this quality. It's all about the individual and how much he or she cares about the work and the organization.

EXAMINE YOUR HIRING CRITERIA.

I'm not suggesting that passion is the only reason to hire someone, but it certainly should be one of the key reasons. When I hire someone, I want them to be "smartly passionate." I'm not talking about their grade point average or where they went to school. I mean they should think on their feet, possess good analytical skills, and grasp new concepts quickly.

During interviews, candidates should be asked what they do in their free time, where they see themselves in twenty years, and who they'd most want to have dinner with in the whole world, dead or alive. If you're a dog food company, do the candidate's answers to these more personal questions suggest a genuine interest in dogs? If you're a law firm, would the candidate want to have dinner with a certain Supreme Court justice or with Madonna?

The benefit of hiring a passionate person is that you're often actually hiring a network of passionate people. In not-for-profits, this network isn't limited to people in a similar field but also includes friends and family. Jonathan, a Do Something employee, told us that "when you hire me, you also hire my mom." He was right; she regularly sends us ideas and suggestions. In addition, his sister joined us as an intern last summer. Even his ex-girlfriend recently sent a potential sponsor our way. How do you spell *team player*? J-o-n-a-t-h-a-n. In a corporation you may not want or need an employee's family as part of your network, but you do want a given employee to access her network of contacts to help the company. She may know a consultant who can contribute on a project. She may have worked with a supplier who would be ideal. She may know a fellow MBA graduate who's perfect for a job opening.

FIND WAYS TO MEASURE PASSION.

All this passion-talk raises the logical question, how does HR identify corporate passion? If you're going to use passion as a criterion in the hiring, firing, and promotions, you need to know what its behavioral manifestations are and how to measure them. It's one thing to be passionate about eliminating world hunger—you can listen to people talk about the issues and hear the fervor in their voices and watch them work and see how much they care about raising funds or staging an event. But what if you work for Ralston Purina? How do you identify the employee who is passionate about filling Fido's bowl?

Verbal enthusiasm. This doesn't mean the employee has to talk nonstop about how much he loves the company or always be "up." But it does mean he usually sounds excited when he speaks about prospective positions or existing projects. It means he talks about what he hopes to do with a clear sense of purpose.

Demonstrable commitment. Anyone can say she is dedicated to hard work or to the company. But what does she do that communicates that she is committed to the organization or to a set of ideals? During the hiring process, a recent graduate applying for a job may have a résumé that shows a history of stellar internships and stellar recommendations. An employee may have a track record of doing the "extra credit" assignment on every project to which she is assigned. How about we stop thinking of this as "extra" and start expecting the extra mile from everyone? Does this candidate use your product or service? Find out—ask her a question about it.

Spokesperson. The highest form of passion isn't talking about something or doing it. It's spreading the word to others. Does this candidate inspire others with his vision for what can be done (without being a Pollyanna)? Does he talk to other people about this company (not this job) and how much he believes in it? Is he already thinking about people and partnerships he'd bring to the table?

AVOID THE TRAP OF FOUNDER ROYALTY.

Well-known not-for-profits often have semi-legendary founders at the helm. Many an organization has done well in large part because of the founder's charisma, her ability to attract attention, secure major donors, and so on. When the founder stays too long, though, dynamic people tend to become discouraged. For one thing, it seems as if they will never be promoted to the top spot. For another, their passion for the cause is often lost in the long shadow cast by the founder. People need a chance to shine on a major stage, which often isn't possible when a founder's presence overwhelms everyone else.

I left the organization I founded, Dress for Success, for this very reason. I had groomed someone talented and passionate to succeed me, and she was waiting in the wings. One night we both spoke at an event, and I had a chance to really see her shine—but also to note that my founder role automatically pulled the spotlight my direction. I made the decision then to get out of her way. I could have stayed forever, but my presence would have limited not only her but others in the organization. My goal was to build a sustainable institution, not a cult. It was time to step aside.

Wendy Kopp and I like to talk about the powerful role of the founder. I suspect that she will be at the helm of Teach For America forever, eventually leaving on a stretcher or in a pine box. But Wendy would be the first person to acknowledge that her charisma isn't overwhelming. One of the biggest inflection points for the organization was when she promoted—and empowered—Jerry Hauser to be its first COO. Powerful COOs are not punishment for founder-CEOs. Wendy was thrilled to have someone to help shoulder the responsibility. In her own words, she was "stretched too thin." Other people in the organization didn't feel demoted because they now had a layer between them and the visionary leader; on the contrary, they were relieved to have the dedicated support necessary to rock their jobs.

Most big companies aren't run by founders, but they often have CEOs and other senior executives who lack the self-awareness to leave or bring in a COO. Instead, they overstay their welcome. People lose their passion when they're convinced that their boss will be there forever and there's no chance that they'll be promoted to that job. Term limits are a good idea for capstone positions. If top executives want to stay with the company, that's fine, but they should stay in some other capacity than the job they've held for years. When people know key jobs will be opening up on a regular basis, the passionate employees are likely to stay and wait for their chance to exhibit their passion.

BE INVENTIVE ABOUT PROMOTIONS.

Being inventive about promotions essentially means redefining what a promotion entails. It is crucial to promote people for their passionate work regularly and meaningfully. If you do so only once in a blue moon, it's not going to have much impact. Unfortunately, even in the largest corporations, plum positions open up infrequently. Therefore it's necessary to find ways to promote people in untraditional ways.

Not-for-profits excel at it. DoSomething.org and other companies often promote people to positions that don't exist on the organizational chart. Suppose someone has worked hard, achieved a lot, and demonstrated a level of zeal that deserves recognition. If there's no opening in the next logical job, we'll frequently create a new job with a new title and new responsibilities.

The reward doesn't necessarily have to be financial (though salary increases and bonuses do send a clear message about what a company values). It doesn't have to be a fancy, familiar title like vice president. But it does have to be meaningful in some way for the person receiving the promotion. Seek input from the potential promotee; ask what type of title he wants, what sort of responsibilities he hopes will come with the promotion. Corporations are sometimes so rigidly tied to their human resources guidelines that they fail to give themselves the freedom to promote inventively. I'm suggesting that they need to loosen up these guidelines.

This doesn't mean promoting people at the drop of a hat and turning promotion into an empty reward. The last thing you want to do is hand out promotions like penny candy at a Fourth of July parade or beads at Mardi Gras. When you expand your range of meaningful promotions, however, you give yourself more ways to communicate to people that you appreciate and encourage their passion.

BE SHOCKINGLY TRANSPARENT.

In corporations an air of secrecy often hovers around promotions. Before someone is actually promoted, rumor and innuendo circulate throughout the office corridors. No one is quite sure why Joe received a promotion and Mary didn't. The boss tells her direct report that she's planning on giving him a promotion in six months but cautions, "Don't let anyone know." And even when Joe's promotion is announced, no one explains why Joe was promoted, and even if Joe knows, he's asked not to go into specifics about why he was named to the position and Mary wasn't. Blah blah blah.

This lack of transparency makes it difficult for the company to communicate that it is rewarding people for their enthusiasm, energy, and gumption. A company may promote the passionate, but no one will be aware of this fact. If a bear plants a flower in the woods, he ought to pick it and bring it into the city with him so other people can smell it too.

Instead of hiding their reasons for giving someone a promotion, organizations should broadcast them loudly and clearly. Send out an internal memo explaining why Joe was chosen for the job; detail that all his late nights on Project X and his willingness to keep trying different approaches until one worked cinched his promotion; mention that his positive attitude and his eagerness to help others marked him as a candidate for the job over a year ago.

Similarly, refrain from sending out boilerplate press releases announcing that Joe has been promoted. Instead, let Joe write or contribute to the writing of the release. Make sure that the release specifies why he received the promotion. In this way, you reinforce the importance of passion in the organization and alert people that this is a key reason why employees get promoted.

LIMIT TEDIUM.

Why does the word *professionalism* often seem synonymous with *boredom*? If you hire and promote a bunch of fantastically passionate people, then lock them up in cubicles and make them suffer endless paperwork and attend countless meetings, you will quickly turn your princes into frogs.

At DoSomething.org we have weekly staff meetings, to which each participant must bring one accomplishment, one goal, and one request. Someone's *accomplishment* can be landing a new sponsor or making a terrific presentation at a conference; or perhaps she had a really restful vacation last week—but doesn't that tell her colleagues something about where her head is? A *goal* can be big, hairy, and audacious; or it can be something for the short run, in which case the employee will have to provide an update the next week, having raised expectations. And the *request* can be made of the group, a particular department, one person, Mother Nature, anything.

The intention is for major departments and individuals to sync both priorities and pain points. People have mutual awareness. Hearing that "that guy who looks like he is always daydreaming" is actually getting stuff done fosters a sense of respect.

Sometimes if we have more than twenty people in our meeting, we'll host it standing up. Literally, everyone standing. This encourages sharp thinking and limits the potential for any one person to blather on and on. One network television president whom I know likes the idea of efficiency from standing so much that he has no chairs in his office.

Weekly check-ins and standing meetings are two simple ways to limit tedium. Every company has a "bummer" element that can be eliminated, whether it's the color of a wall, an operating procedure, or an actual person. Cut out that cancer. If you want your company to be a place where passion rules the roost, you've got to consistently and vigilantly make sure that every element reinforces that goal.

ELEVEN QUESTIONS TO GET YOU STARTED:
Do More with Your Staff

Back in the ginormous company's conference room, I'm wondering: Suppose I sent out an e-mail to the talented, experienced people in this room (that is, every one of them, no doubt), announcing the creation of a new task force to work on a new project. It would involve more hours and more challenges but no additional compensation—in fact, it might eat up some of their vacation time. Would anyone attend the meeting? That would be a great test of passion in a workplace.

I once asked my office manager to send this note around my office. (I didn't want it to come from me, for fear people would show up suspecting it was a test of loyalty to the boss, when it was actually a measure of love for the workplace itself.) Nearly the entire organization showed up for the meeting, notepad in hand and curious smile on face. The people who weren't in the room? Exactly who I expected . . . and they were on my short list to go.

Look around and ask yourself these eleven questions:

1. Does your staff wear their company swag? On free time? Are they jogging in the park wearing your company T-shirt?

2. What role does your founder play in your company? Feared father figure? Beloved and sacred ghost? Are people there to serve that legacy or the corporate purpose? Are those two things in conflict?

3. Does your workplace see the display of emotion as a weakness? Do people ever sigh and say how proud they are to be part of the team, or would that be viewed as frail—or, worse yet, as not genuine?

4. Is your team lean? Do they feel "overworked" or "really busy"?

5. Do people sacrifice for your company? Do they steal office supplies to take home—or do they bring items from home to the office? Has anyone ever brought in a sibling to help for the day?

6. In the interview process, do you ask candidates if they use your product or service? Do you ask them why or why not? Do you ask them how they spend their free time—and then measure that against your corporate brand?

7. Do your employees speak passionately about your brand? Do their actions reflect passion? Does their word of mouth as ambassadors inspire others?

8. How do you structure your staff meetings? Does the same person run the meeting each week? Is there a consistent format that includes fun, a chance for all to speak, and the opportunity for new items to be mentioned?

9. Have you ever hired someone who made no sense on paper but was simply superpassionate about the company? Do you have a George?

10. Is being at your company for a long time seen as an asset, as job security? Or is producing results the ultimate criterion? When was the last time a long-term employee was fired?

11. Are promotions routine—scheduled, according to a clear track? Or can people leapfrog and excel as a result of performance, regardless of tradition?

DO MORE WITH YOUR STORY

YOU KNOW THIS GINORMOUS company I keep telling you about? I have to confess that I actually love the thing it makes. A lot of other people I know love it too. The ad campaigns are always quite fabulous, and the logo appears in the background at lots of sporting events and concerts. One of the many things that ran through my head as I sat in that meeting, listening to all those ad people freak out about their shrinking budget, was, *Who came up with their product, the thing that everybody loves so much?* After thinking about it for a while, I realized that I had no idea. I knew nothing about the origins of this product or of this company, and that struck me as weird.

Storytelling is the antithesis of corporate efficiency. Storytelling is emotional and personal. Sometimes a story involves luck or coincidence. Often it can be messy. None of those adjectives are found on a corporate wish list.

Some companies seem to forget that they even have stories. In the professional, buttoned-down world, it's easy to overlook how

the founder crushed the competition and was brilliantly effective, if somewhat ruthless, in establishing the organization. It's also understandable that, at a certain point in time, the company's leadership decided it was time to look forward, not back, and to focus on the future. The emotional stories are especially difficult to talk about— the ones about how the company's products and services failed for years and then finally something happened and everything changed. It's messy. It's complicated. It's often seen as retrospective and not in a positive way.

Typically, employees and customers hear only a well-crafted message about the organization. It's screened and sanitized, polished and professional. Sometimes it's not even authentic, a mere concoction of a branding consultant with a vivid imagination and a knack for a catchy phrase. This is fine, for what it's worth (usually far less than what the company paid the consultant to come up with it), but what is sacrificed are the 101 great stories from the company's past and the one great story that describes the company's future. The thing that's often forgotten—by leadership, by ad agencies, by staff—is that these stories aren't just entertainment; they provide stakeholders with a sense of the organization as a living, breathing organism. They help people identify with it, empathize with it, and be inspired by it. They enable people to see the humanity in the organization.

Humanity is often missing from corporate communications, be they press releases or memos or even annual reports, which have pretty pictures but dull prose that lacks even a hint of vividness. At times it seems as if a corporate communications department couldn't create buzz among stakeholders if it released a swarm of bees into a field of roses.

Why does it matter? I've heard the people at this ginormous company complain that quarterly earnings are down, that layoffs are looming, and that this media budget was just the latest unexpected slash. And yet I realized that while I love the product, I knew nothing about the company's heart—only its calloused hands and feet. I knew nothing about its creation story or how far it had come

from wherever it started. I wanted to feel sorry for these staffers, to join in their coterie of discontent, but lacking knowledge of the corporate personality, I had nothing to grasp but incessant whining.

I'm not going to tell you that storytelling is a panacea for corporate pain, or a silver-bullet solution for whatever ails the modern company. I am going to tell you that, in not-for-profits, storytelling makes a huge difference. Stories are the glue that helps employees unite within their organization. They provide a context for the company and its operations—a sense of past, present, and future that helps stakeholders appreciate the company's trajectory over time as well as its successes, failures, and all the other in-betweens that have led to today.

Sometimes stories are the only way we know about a cause. We learn about the Holocaust by reading Anne Frank's diary or Elie Wiesel's autobiographical *Night*. We better understand the plight of apartheid by hearing the story of Nelson Mandela. How would we get real insight into the tragedy in Haiti without the stories brought out by people who survived?

Most companies, thankfully, have happier stories than these tragic examples, even in the worst of times. Theirs may be stories of epiphany or innovation, of wild risk, teamwork, or collaboration, of triumphs and setbacks—all these are your stories. Cost? Zilch. Deployed correctly and cleverly, these stories will make your employee pride skyrocket, differentiate your brand from its competitors, give your customers a feeling of connection to you, and connect you to the past in such a way as to give what you do today a bit more context and a bit more meaning.

Think about the story of Hewlett-Packard's founding. In 1939 two guys created the company in their Palo Alto, California, garage. People love this story. More than seventy years later, it still resonates because it feels homespun. It reminds people of the company's entrepreneurial, seat-of-its-pants spirit. HP may make machines, but its genesis story gives it a soul. Hewlett-Packard is the company that was founded in that garage. It's even used that image in its advertising—and President Obama frequently cites HP as an

example of small-business success. Got that? The president of the United States grasped the founding story of a private company and cited it in speeches intended to spur American businesses to dream again. Nice free advertising, eh?

Which stories are important and which are tangential? How do you identify and communicate the stories that would have the greatest effect on your organization internally as well as out in the marketplace? And how do you use all of today's media to create buzz around the story you want to tell? Let's turn to the not-for-profit world for some answers.

HONOR YOUR GENESIS STORY.

In the beginning. Three powerful words. Virtually every ancient culture had an oral tradition or a written scripture that recorded a creation story. Humans want to know their roots. We want to know where we came from. We want to understand where we've been.

Not-for-profits brilliantly use "founder folklore" to position their brand in the marketplace. Darell Hammond, founder of Ka-BOOM!, which creates community play spaces (see Chapter 6), tells the story of how he grew up with his eight siblings in Mooseheart Child City and School, a group home just west of Chicago. Darell recounts his favorite childhood pastimes of skipping rocks and hanging in the Mooseheart playground. To an outsider, it might sound like a hard-luck story, but Darell says he felt lucky for the warm volunteers who kept that place going and grateful to have a place to play and just be a kid.

Years later Darell read an article about two children who had suffocated in an abandoned car because they had nowhere else to play. He knew he needed to act. Opportunities for play had allowed him to survive and thrive, so Darell and his friend Dawn Hutchison decided to build playgrounds. Their first playground, located in a housing project called Livingston Manor in Southeast D.C., involved an honorary seven-year-old project manager and helped

unify a fractured community. A *Washington Post* article perpetu-
ated the excitement and pushed the budding organization into the
limelight. It mentioned Darell's personal history. It was then that
KaBOOM! was named and Home Depot signed on as the first
funding partner.

Darell's story is the gas that originally fueled the engine of
KaBOOM! His personal trajectory is compelling, vivid, acces-
sible, and most important, authentic. It is the inspiration behind
KaBOOM!'s various communications, which exude his heartfelt
belief in the ebullience—and importance—of play. Volunteers
know about him. Employees breathe his air. Donors are converted
by him. And the media want to repeat his story. It all helps create
what Darell refers to as "inside-out radiance," and a glow of joy and
authenticity emerges from it. His story is what makes KaBOOM!
go boom! It differentiates his organization from the rest of the not-
for-profit field. And it confers genuineness and extra meaning on
an organization that could, in less colorful terms, be described as
a construction group. Without the story, it's a company that builds
playgrounds. With the story of how the founder found happiness
through play, it's one that tries to bring joy to a new generation of
kids. The story of the founder becomes the creation story of the
organization.

A founder's story can take on a life of its own, becoming gospel
even without a PR person pounding on reporters' doors or making
much of a deliberate effort to communicate it. I know because it
happened to me—and only then did I fully understand the power of
storytelling. I never intended to use my own story of founding Dress
for Success to help the organization prosper. But when a *New York
Times* reporter wrote a story about how I inherited $5,000 from my
immigrant great-grandfather and used it to start the organization,
the story resonated with a lot of people.

Poppy Max was the sixth boy in his family. They all lived in
Poland, and back around the turn of the century it was the law that
when Jewish males turned eighteen, they were conscripted into the
army for twenty years. His family knew this would be the fate of the

five older brothers. So when Max was born, they hid his existence. He never had a birth certificate or formal papers. He never went to school. He never celebrated a birthday. And when he reached puberty (nobody is sure exactly how old he was, because nobody remembered when he'd been born), they sneaked him onto a boat headed for America.

Since Poppy Max didn't know his birth date, the immigration officer at Ellis Island assigned him December 25, figuring he'd never forget it. Two weeks later he found a distant cousin who loaned him a pushcart. That's how my Poppy Max became a peddler. He was the guy who could get you whatever you needed, a sort of professional scrambler and a precursor to today's personal shopper. Looking for a nice wedding ring to propose to your girl? Max could get it cheap. Need to find some kosher pickles to sell at your store? He'd get you the best. At one point he was the king of bath mats. For me, needless to say, it was a bit strange—and totally humbling—to inherit $5,000 from a man who had come to America with nothing and worked so hard to scrape together enough to support his family and to build a life.

So thanks to his hard work, there I was at twenty-three years old, cold and wet from the February rain, just waiting for the elevator to take me to my tiny warm apartment, with an unexpected check for $5,000 in my hands. I knew I had to do something to honor his memory. I was a miserable law student at the time. Those classes were so theoretical, impersonal. Most of my classmates just wanted to land a top mark, a spot on law review, and then a high-paying job at a fancy corporate firm. Chilly, dripping in misery, holding that check, I had an epiphany: the idea for Dress for Success came to me right there, in the elevator. I saw it as a way to help women reclaim their destinies, much as the United States helped my great-grandfather start a new life.

Even though this story says nothing about women's suits or job interviews, it was the Dress for Success creation story. It is the organization's genesis tale. And Dress for Success became inextricably and wonderfully linked with my story about Poppy Max and

me the unhappy law student. It was perfect because it communicated how anything is possible, that from humble beginnings great and unexpected things can emerge. Like Darell Hammond's story, it provided our fledgling organization with authenticity and differentiation.

What makes these stories great is their mixture of hope and tragedy, risk and renewal. Rodrigo Mendes runs a program in Brazil that uses art to help disabled children process their emotions, communicate with people, and just have fun. Rodrigo himself is paralyzed from the neck down. When he tells his personal story, how he came to be in that chair and later create this wonderful organization, he doesn't begin by saying that one night when he was eighteen years old, he was mugged and shot on the streets of Brazil. Instead, he smiles and tells you how he loved to play soccer. And that he was actually quite good. He explains that his former dream was to be a surgeon. By giving these details, he simultaneously disarms the listener, letting us feel that he was once just like them—and yet this background makes it clear how able-bodied his life and dreams once were. He humanizes himself. His personal story makes listeners think about what he—and all the disabled children he works with—has lost and also found. Knowing him and his story makes us want to help his program thrive.

Smart not-for-profits integrate their genesis story into every aspect of the company, from the website to events to internal communications. You don't want to turn it into your broken record— you don't want to tell that story yourself, in the exact same words, so many times that people roll their eyes as soon as you start in on it—but you do want to make sure that the story is documented, respected, and repeated.

The Girl Scouts, which turns one hundred in 2012, has done a good job of honoring its founder, Juliette "Daisy" Gordon Low, yet not overdoing it so that today's Brownies and Scouts feel as if they are camping with her ghost. They have turned Daisy's home into a museum in Savannah, Georgia, named an award for her, and even published biographies of her. They've struck a good

balance between respecting their history and focusing on today's organization.

The for-profit sector has seen plenty of compelling founders' tales—stories of innovation and creativity and chutzpah. Makeup artist Bobbi Brown started her own cosmetics line because she was frustrated by the lack of options for women of color. Ray Kroc was a salesman who happened to make a sales call on a restaurant in California run by the McDonald brothers. Pierre Omidyar infamously founded eBay because he wanted to find PEZ dispensers for his wife's collection, right? Actually, this story was recently debunked as a corporate fairy tale . . . but it worked!

A few common threads run through all these stories. Most companies had humble beginnings. Most companies had a founder or founders with a vision that was inspired by a personal experience. Most start-up stories involve a great idea but also great (exciting) risk.

All the for-profit examples I cited above led to amazing things— value creation, enormous profit, huge success. Understanding a founding moment can make a global gargantuan into something anyone can appreciate. People want to work and do business with companies that possess a human face. The founder's tale may not achieve this goal in and of itself, but it will push the company toward it.

TELL POSTGENESIS STORIES TOO.

While the founder story is the most obvious tale worth telling, many other stories exist within an organization that should become part of its brand, strategy, and culture.

Not-for-profits are masters at uncovering such stories and at understanding which ones to tell to employees, to donors, to volunteers, and to the media in order to get out the word about the organization's effectiveness and reach. Some stories work better in small settings or help illustrate a particular kind of challenge, while others

show the heart of a company. It's not as if they have gone through an actual vetting process. Rather, they have risen to the top of historical memory as people have told them and heard them told. They are so good and so apropos that people naturally repeat them.

John Lilly, CEO of Mozilla, might well be called the group's CES—Chief Executive Storyteller. He values stories as a way to boost the brand, and he tells them well and often. One of his best involves a man he met named Naji, who grew up in Mongolia but went to school in northern Germany and wanted to keep in touch with his parents in Mongolia via e-mail. While northern Germany isn't exactly a developing country with poor technology, he had no software that could connect him easily and freely. Naji downloaded Firefox and localized the Mozilla tools for Mongolia, making it possible for twenty thousand Mongolians to access this software every day. Coding and translating Internet software is far from glamorous work, and in this case it didn't affect a huge number of people. But the people it did affect had their communications transformed. For that group of Web-enabled Mongolians—and for Naji and his relatives—it was vitally important.

What does this story accomplish? On the most basic level, it might make a Mozilla employee or volunteer feel good about being part of the organization. On a financial level, it might inspire a donation—or on a lucky day with the right listener, even a large donation. But the real value is that the story captures and communicates Mozilla's purpose in a memorable, compelling way. Naji's ability to access Mozilla's tools and adapt them to his personal needs proves that Mozilla's brand and philosophy transcend national boundaries. Its product reaches across the globe, even into the far corners of Europe and Asia. Can you imagine a better story to illustrate Mozilla's dedication to universal Internet access?

It's much easier to identify a genesis story (it happened at the beginning!) than to dig up Naji tales. A company that has been in business for years and has thousands of employees is probably overflowing with stories—stories about everything from a major takeover to how that crazy guy in IT created a really weird screen saver.

Capturing and extracting the key ones is the challenge. Does your company have a mechanism or person who is responsible for collecting these examples?

One of the most popular, effective genres is stories about how the organization overcame a crisis. Many times these stories reflect organizational values—how leaders stood firm in the face of adversity or displayed courage and initiative to overcome major challenges. Wendy Kopp will talk about the time (more than one time, actually) when Teach For America almost went broke—which seems shocking now, in the face of its awesome success and its growth into one of the most popular recruiters of college graduates in America. Knowing that more than once the organization had trouble making payroll transforms Wendy the icon to Wendy the mere mortal who once struggled like the rest of us but had a dream and never gave up.

We also like to identify success stories. One tells how a former Dress for Success client ended up in the human resource department at a bank and created a program to hire other women in transition from welfare to work. Another tells how a fifty-year-old janitor learned to read as a result of the adult education program at the school he cleaned—and then landed a job as a writer for the local newspaper.

Every organization has significant people stories as well as crisis-recovery stories. Find them. Tell them. Make them known. They serve to remind your employees that their work really does affect the lives of others. And they make outsiders relate to your people, product, and brand. These stories make people feel compassion and loyalty, as they can distinguish you from your competitors. And these stories stick with people, who remember them and your company.

CREATE A CULTURE OF STORYTELLING.

Our data-driven times place a premium on charts and statistics, concrete measures and airtight metrics. There's nothing wrong with

them—to the contrary, they're essential for gauging performance and effectiveness. But we shouldn't underestimate the value of anecdotal evidence either. Those stories, such as the explanation of how one person's life was dramatically changed as a result of an organization's services, matter.

Doctors Without Borders is the renowned international organization that works to bring medical care to people in crisis. It goes to the world's hot spots, to places where doctors don't normally work and where hospitals are rare at best. Doctors Without Borders has some impressive statistics about how quickly it can parachute into a certain war zone (four hours) and how many patients it has saved (millions). But it's more compelling, more powerful, and more accessible to hear a doctor's firsthand account of the time he saved the life of a woman—who had walked two days to reach help, despite the war raging around her and a baby attached to her hip—by performing surgery to stop the internal bleeding she sustained after being raped by warlords. Think you'll remember that one?

In the last few years microfinance organizations have flourished. Is it because loan recipients are, studies show, defaulting less on their repayments? Is it because Muhammad Yunus, the founder of the pioneering Grameen Bank in Bangladesh, won a Nobel Peace Prize for the ways he has reshaped finance for the least privileged? Is it because organizations like the Acumen Fund, Kiva, and ACCION are now able to use multimedia to tell their stories less clinically and more emotionally? I'd say all three, but it's the third that seems to me to be pointing to the future.

We're now able to see photos or perhaps a video of the woman in Guatemala who would like to buy a sewing machine so that she can mend clothing and earn a living. Months later, after we help her get it, we can check to see how her business is progressing. We're no longer sending money "over there"; we're investing in actual people and their dreams.

Too often for-profit companies use media and websites to tout statistics about same-store sales growth or quarterly profits, market dominance, or some other really-difficult-to-understand-on-a-

human-level-but-surely-impressive achievement. This is perfectly natural—your new product is driving sales, so of course you talk about it! My suggestion? Don't limit the discussion to facts and figures. Use all the tools at your disposal to tell the stories behind the numbers.

Not-for-profits use knowledge-management systems for disseminating stories, not just data. This is the simplest way to communicate them to staff. When people are searching for information on emerging markets or acquisition strategies, they shouldn't receive only quantitative data—studies, statistics, and so on. The company should capture and store relevant stories from current and former employees with expertise in a given area and share these qualitative anecdotes with the staff. These stories can bring to life some of those dry numbers and provide insights that data may be incapable of conveying.

Share stories from the field. Stories from the trenches aren't as big as leadership stories or stories of monumental events in the company's past, but they're still significant. Tell the story of how a salesperson landed a big account or how a tech team revolutionized the company's information systems. Tell stories from customers that demonstrate the quality of a product or the superiority of service. American Express has always used the stories of innovators and entrepreneurs—famous and not-so-famous—in their advertising campaigns. From celebrity Ellen DeGeneres and director Martin Scorsese to Warren Brown, who started a bakery called CakeLove in Washington, D.C., AmEx uses their images to demonstrate that they are the card for passionate dreamers. The AmEx story is *their* story, and potentially *your* story.

Use in-house media to establish story-based institutional memory. Every company has a history. No matter how young your company is, it's important to record it. That history is often lost because no one is bothering to write it down. You've probably heard the saying, "Those who forget the past are condemned to repeat it." Well, stories can catalog mistakes as well as successes, providing yellow flags about dangerous strategies and tactics. And they

can also preserve the company's larger story, from its founding to its evolution over the years to its current state and how it's rooted in that history.

Institutional memory grounds a company in events but also in values and beliefs. History demonstrates that a company was built on a clear and explicable foundation. All too easily everyone— from employees to financial analysts—forgets that the organization evolved from a base of core values and ideas. When people view a place through a historical lens, they are much better able to understand its policies and practices.

I'm not suggesting that everyone in your company sit around in circles, swapping stories, passing peace pipes, and inhaling the wisdom of their elders. If they do that all day, not much is going to get done. And you can't load up your website with a gazillion stories and expect people to benefit from them all. You have to use common sense. Be selective about your storytelling. A few great stories are far superior to a score of good ones. Some stories may deliver the right message but do so in dull or ordinary ways. Hunt down stories that will stick in people's minds because they're so dramatic, humorous, or unusual. Some stories may really be memorable but tangential to your brand. Avoid them as well. The most effective kind of story will reflect your *first, only, faster, better,* or *cheaper* statement.

Look for stories that make you feel and also make you think. It's easier to evoke an emotional response when you're talking about raising money for AIDS and babies than for park benches or libraries. It might be about an employee who takes so much pride in his job that he stayed up two nights in a row until he solved a problem facing his team. It might be about how two people in a group were constantly in conflict but were the only ones available to run operations during a blizzard, making every delivery on time. It might be about a customer who had a life-changing epiphany as a result of using your product. Whatever the story, tell it with characters and detail, so the listener knows that he is listening to a story, not a lesson.

CREATE BUZZ ON A BUDGET OF ZERO.

Here's a confession: I don't really "get" professional football, and I especially don't understand the Super Bowl. The strange hand signals, the rushing right into a pile of big fat men, the plays that seem to yield nothing but the beginnings of long-term brain damage, and particularly the companies that spend millions of dollars on thirty seconds of ad time—when most people are taking a bathroom break.

I've always wondered whether ad execs confuse having a spot air during the Super Bowl with actually playing in the Super Bowl. You might win awards for your fancy overpriced ad, but nobody is going to give you a ring or invite you to the White House to celebrate it. Most people don't even know what a Cannes Lions is. The ads might be discussed at work the next day or receive a mention on the breakfast news, but even then it's not entirely obvious whether those spots actually lead to increased sales adequate to justify the huge expense.

Companies don't have to spend that kind of money to generate buzz, and they certainly don't have to hire an outside creative firm to concoct some cockamamie story about Clydesdale horses. Instead they can look within, to the people who work there and who probably have a wealth of stories that would do the trick. Do you ask your employees for anecdotal evidence of success each quarter? Do you ask them to write down examples of how your product or service affected a customer's life? Do you keep those love letters from happy customers—or does someone in HR just send them a polite thank-you and a coupon?

Valuing anecdotal evidence, collecting those stories, and telling them well is only the first part of creating a not-for-profit storytelling culture. If a bear tells a story in the woods and nobody is there to hear it, does it matter? Organizations need to figure out how to generate an audience for these messages.

Zainab Salbi, CEO of Women for Women International, which works mostly in postconflict regions, wrote a book to tell her story.

Kate Roberts, the founder of YouthAIDS, speaks at conferences and lectures at universities. Billy Shore, CEO of Share Our Strength, an organization that battles child hunger, uses his personal blog to share stories that relate to his brand. None of these people sent out a press release and then sat waiting for some journalist to pick up his or her story and run with it. Instead they created the media they wanted to see. They recognized that the art of storytelling isn't just the story—it's also the telling and the retelling.

The most nimble not-for-profits are especially smart about using Web-based tools such as Twitter and Facebook to generate excitement about what they're doing. And it doesn't cost much money.

Charity: water was one of the first not-for-profit organizations to really embrace the Twitter culture. As staff members registered for Twitter one after the other, the close-knit crew thought seriously about how they could use it to bolster their cause. At first the charity: water team used Twitter much in the same way anyone else would: followers received updates about staff members' travel schedules, their meetings, even their lunch breaks. As mundane as these matters may seem, they help tell the charity: water story, which is one of a strong work ethic and fresh thinkers. With more than a million Twitter followers, the organization doesn't need to push out a press release or beg CNN to tell its story—its following *is* the media it wants to see.

Social media allow you to spread a story faster than ever before among a global population. Just as significantly, these communications technologies allow you to tell your story in your own words. The problem with sending out a news release about your story is that it gets filtered by hundreds of pairs of editorial eyes, and before you know it, the story that emerges isn't really the story you want to tell. For instance, when Cameron Sinclair of Architecture for Humanity writes a blogpost for *The Huffington Post*, he can tell the organization's story in his desired words and reap the benefits of a site that now has over 30 million unique users per month.

REMEMBER THAT AN IMAGE IS EVERYTHING.

We're living in a visual world. That famous televised debate, after which Richard Nixon lost the presidential election to John F. Kennedy because he was a sweaty mess, was just fifty years ago—a millisecond in history, but it seems like aeons ago. Ever since, we've been obsessed with image, with visuals, with looks.

Not-for-profits have learned this lesson. (Maybe not from Nixon, but still . . .) We get it: a good picture is worth a gazillion words. One powerful image can indelibly impress itself on people's minds and create tremendous talk and discussion. At not-for-profits, we know the power of an image—a starving child, a diminishing glacier, an oil slick on a pristine body of water. I'm not discounting the power of words—after all, this book is filled with more than sixty thousand of them—but I am advocating the inclusion of visual elements whenever possible. This is especially true when using websites to communicate stories, since they allow us to integrate photos and video and to change them often, at a minimal expense.

Not-for-profits have been really smart about loading tons of images into free open sites like Flickr. Its helps our cause to have tons of images out there making our point. Entering the word *endangered* reveals more than seventy-five thousand images on Flickr. Organizations and activists have uploaded thousands of photos of cute and cuddly but little-known species like the Philippine tarsier or the Mexican wolf. Seeing these photos might make even a professional trapper think twice.

Recently PETA uploaded some videos on YouTube that an undercover employee took on a cell phone at a slaughterhouse. We've all heard (and tried to forget) the data and the stories of mistreatment of our food animals. But those images turned me vegan for a few weeks, and I'm still not sure I'll ever be able to eat a cheeseburger with the same gusto.

Has your company made the most of the free outlets available to generate buzz, lasting impressions, and viral visual representations?

CHOOSE THE MESSENGER.

Who is telling the story? Whether you're the CEO of a Fortune 500 company or the executive director of a not-for-profit, the general public probably doesn't know who you are. (Sorry.) And even if the public knows your name, do people really want to listen to you? I think I'm funny, and my grandmother always tells me I look snazzy, but I'm smart enough to know that there are people out there who are potentially much more effective at delivering our message than I will ever be, even on a good hair day. A genetically gifted (and some-times artificially enhanced) celebrity has a platform, a recognizable face, and often a distinctive voice. She can differentiate a story. She can be a megaphone. A well-known individual, especially a live per-former, can also likely tell a story better than most.

Not-for-profits have learned how to make star power shine some tinted light our way. Marlo Thomas has been a terrific, credible, moving spokesperson for St. Jude's Children's Research Hospital, which was founded by her late father. Sally Struthers did a great job in commercials for the Christian Children's Fund—so much so that in millions of American minds her name is now irrevocably linked to those sad, plaintive, malnourished children. Nick Jonas of the Jonas Brothers has changed how people think about juvenile diabetes and has raised millions for the cause. But my favorite ex-ample is actually David Arquette and the work he does for Feeding America.

In 2008 America's Second Harvest, the nation's largest coali-tion of food pantries, changed its name to Feeding America. Name changes are really tough for not-for-profits. The clients weren't going anywhere—they still needed the food kitchens—but would the "customers" remain? Would the donors, volunteers, and others who were connected to the brand America's Second Harvest still recognize it as something else? Feeding America knew it needed an aggressive, proactive approach during the shift. One element of the strategy was to build a celebrity team that could participate in events, help attract cameras, and publicize the new name as well as the mis-

sion. Now I know what you're thinking: David Arquette? Isn't he most famous for being married to Courteney Cox? Well, he may not ever win an Oscar for those *Scream* movies or grace the cover of *Vanity Fair*, but he recently spent several days locked in a glass box, suspended in the air, as a means of raising money for the organization. It's tough to get most celebrities to show up to an event for ten minutes to smile on the red carpet—yet Arquette gave three entire days of his life. More important than his dozens of appearances and events for the organization, this guy is rumored to work his Black-Berry for Feeding America like a twelve-year-old girl calling a local radio station for Miley Cyrus tickets. He is relentless.

How brilliant of Feeding America to think of celebrities as not just pretty faces that preen for cameras. They've given David the sound bites and stories and asked him for something very specific: recruit your friends. He is the kind of person who rubs the genie's lamp and, with his one wish, asks for three more wishes.

David is the captain of a large campaign to keep Feeding America and the current epidemic food shortage in the headlines. He utilizes his star power and connections to make sure that story stays out there. Branding and public relations expert Shawn Sachs of Sunshine, Sachs & Associates calls David "the quarterback. And just like a Manning brother, you build the team around him."

Do the celebrities you use show up for the day of your print shoot and then are never seen again? Is your storyteller a true believer? Have you armed him or her with more than just talking points and statistics—with a reason to care? Using celebrities well doesn't require hiring a fancy agency or opening an office in Los Angeles (though those steps can help). Find someone who loves your product, and enlist his or her help.

ACT FAST.

Sometimes *when* we tell our story is just as important as *what* our story is. Successful not-for-profits tend to be fast-acting enterprises,

especially when it comes to grabbing free media opportunities. We respond quickly to public events if they give us a window for telling a particular story, making our brand relevant, or launching a campaign. When opportunity knocks, we open the door with our coat and shoes on, ready to go.

In February 2009, on the eve of the Grammy Awards ceremony in Los Angeles, entertainer Chris Brown made headlines for beating his then girlfriend, the pop sensation Rihanna, in a Lamborghini. For a few days the gossip and gruesome photo evidence dominated the news and online chatter. Here were two role models for young people, but shockingly, no organization was helping those young people figure out how they should confront similar situations in their own lives. Do Something had never addressed the issue of teen dating violence, but somebody had to step up. We decided to shoot a video reenactment of the incident to show people what teen dating abuse looks like and to highlight the fact that one in three teens will be in a violent relationship.

An intern recruited two friends from New York University to be our actors. They took the subway to the Lamborghini dealership in Midtown, and while one of our staff distracted the dealer-owner, the kids leaped into a car and the intern used her handheld camera to shoot the reenactment according to the timeline and details laid out in the LAPD report. It cost us approximately twenty dollars (to have the DVD translated into a code format that the TV networks were requesting for news programs), and it had over one million YouTube views. For two nights in a row our Chris Brown–Rihanna reenactment story was the lead on entertainment news programs. It made the *Today* show and scores of blogs. If we had waited even a day or two longer, we would not have had nearly as much buzz.

We took a leap, instead of sitting and writing a plan. "Reacting quickly" isn't a public relations strategy for everyone or every situation. But people in your company should be empowered to react quickly on behalf of the brand.

Frankly, in the age of Twitter and YouTube, your customers are reacting quickly to mice in your restaurant and to typos in your

store window signage—those photos are online within minutes. Sometimes quick action isn't about taking advantage of a moment, it's about reacting to a story you didn't intend to be out there. Can you keep up?

USE MULTIPLE MECHANISMS TO TELL YOUR STORY.

In this chapter I've talked a lot about being the media you want to see, using Twitter, YouTube, Facebook, Flickr, and other free technologies to tell your story, project an image, and monitor how others are framing your story.

But I don't want to ignore traditional media as a way of communicating a story. Having a trusted resource feature your company can give your story huge credibility. In what the Columbia School of Journalism refers to the "*60 Minutes* effect," an appearance on the high-profile show can have a huge impact on an organization. And as everyone knows, an appearance on *Oprah*—or even the briefest positive mention by the queen of daytime talk—can launch a brand into the stratosphere, turning an unknown story into something on every housewife's lips. Having appeared on *Oprah* and witnessed this effect firsthand, I can testify that it's totally true. (The funny part is that you never know when your episode will run as a repeat. So one day you're sitting there, at the end of an afternoon, and all of the sudden you're flooded by e-mails and calls at 4 P.M., 5 P.M., and then 6 P.M. And it hits you, *Ah. We re-aired on* Oprah *today across the country*.

The competition to appear on such high-profile shows is intense, and not many CEOs have the chance or the story to be *Oprah* guests. The point isn't that corporate leaders should try and break into talk-show green rooms, but that they should be willing, eager, and able to appear in whatever media forums are available. Corporate leaders can think of lots of reasons not to appear: they don't want the competition to know what they're up to; whatever they say could be misinterpreted or challenged by a hostile interviewer; they

prefer to keep a low profile. But the good to be reaped by telling your story far outweighs the bad. If that story is the right one and it's well told, it can capture the hearts and minds of far more stakeholders than ever read the annual report.

ELEVEN QUESTIONS TO GET YOU STARTED:
Do More with Your Story

Since time immemorial, people have loved to tell stories. It's the way we've connected, not just with each other but also with our ancestors. It's been how we explain phenomena that we can't otherwise understand. It's what we use to bring order and history to our little corners of this big, puzzling universe.

Modern storytelling has certain characteristics. We tend to like triumphant endings. We appreciate a good arc. We root for the underdog. We enjoy being surprised. We like clever phrasing and innovative methods.

Good not-for-profits realize all these things. We've done a wise job of selecting our stories and telling them . . . loudly, artfully, and repeatedly. The best part is that telling your story often doesn't cost a dime. Today we have a diversity of storytelling media at our disposal, from the Web to television to radio to print to mobile technology. Using the right techniques, we can exploit all these platforms at little to no cost.

For-profit organizations have no shortage of compelling history. Some corporate-genesis stories have even become like adult bedtime stories—folklore, heroic tales that are told over and over (and sometimes embellished). We love hearing about Michael Dell in his dorm room. We love that Richard Branson dropped out of school to start his Virgin record label. And the Bill Gates story—starting with him dropping out of Harvard—has been

fodder for several books and even became a popular made-for-TV movie.

But there are many more corporate stories that I want to hear. I want to hear the Target story. I want to know why I should care about Pepsi more than Coca-Cola. I want to understand where Cisco Systems came from and why its logo is a bridge. It's a matter of promotion, of course, but it's also a matter of trust. Don't be afraid to tell people what's behind your brand. The benefits of doing so just might astound you.

Here are eleven questions to inspire you to think differently about leveraging the power in your (free) story:

1. What is your company's genesis tale? Who is your founder? What personal pain or experience inspired him or her to create this product or service?

2. Has your company experienced arcs of success and failure? What key people or sacrifices or twists of fate are worth illuminating?

3. Do you collect positive customer-feedback stories? Where are those letters and e-mails? Are they compelling?

4. Is your company's success simply a story of data and dollars? Or can you measure it by noting that specific people celebrated a milestone in your restaurant or that your airline made possible an emergency surgery because it flew to that remote part of the world.

5. Do you control your own media? Are you the media you want to see? Are you using Twitter, Facebook, MySpace,

YouTube, Wikipedia, and Flickr to tell your story, in your own selected words and images?

6. Do you Google your own company? Do you buy ad words to make sure that the first thing that comes up in a search is the story you prefer to be told?

7. Is there a celebrity who loves your product or service? Maybe he's not the most famous or attractive person, but he's a fanatical fan. Are you using him to spread the word?

8. Are your leaders also your chief storytellers? Or are they robots who wear fancy suits and spew data?

9. Do you tell stories about your company or just react to the ones other people tell?

10. If your CEO had the chance to appear on *Oprah*, what would he or she talk about with Oprah? (Hint: Oprah doesn't really care about last quarter's earnings or that you've moved production offshore.)

11. What story is your competition telling?

DO MORE WITH YOUR FINANCES

IT ALMOST SEEMS COUNTERINTUITIVE, doesn't it? How can not-for-profits advise moneymaking corporations about finances? What we do with our money is completely different from what for-profits do. Our goal isn't to maximize profit. We don't have the same concept of the bottom line. Return on investment is gauged with another set of metrics altogether. And while we say we'd like to work ourselves into obsolescence—wouldn't it be nice if we really did solve all of the world's problems?—realistically, we've got no exit on the horizon . . . ever. So why should you listen to us?

Plenty of reasons. Thinking about the financial constructs, the traditions, and the ethos characteristic of not-for-profit organizations is worthwhile precisely because we're such foreign entities. There are often lessons to be learned from the experiences of those who are *unlike* you. And especially in a period of global financial instability, perhaps wisdom can be found in the experiences of organizations that, for years, have had to confront fiscal shakiness.

Is your company struggling to cut costs? Are you trying to impose policies and practices that keep managers accountable for their spending? Have you had to cope with destructive infighting between groups over budgets? When things are good, these issues may seem like mere hiccups, little bumps on a typically smooth path to yet another record-breaking quarter of profits. But when things aren't so good, when your business is suffering, the fundamental, long-term solutions that not-for-profits use with great success may interest you. At the very least I hope that we can introduce you to a new way of thinking about your finances.

I'm guessing that to meet the pressure for profit, your company has imposed all sorts of controls—new rules about co-signatures and approvals for expenses, more explicit budget processes, and the like. Maybe some of these efforts have effectively helped maximize revenues and minimize expenses. I slogged my way through law school, so I'm a huge fan of sound written procedures and careful processes (read: paperwork). But has a new form ever radically changed a workplace for the better?

Corporate finance is complicated stuff, and I'm not going to pretend that not-for-profits possess financial software systems, forecasting models, or fiscal measurement tools that can revolutionize your hedge fund's latest structured finance scheme. I'm also not going to suggest that we confront exactly the same kind of challenges. But what we do know in our world is fiscal responsibility. The sector that doesn't focus on profit is actually quite good at not losing money. We know about living within our means and planning for the future.

LIVE IN FEAR OF OVERHEAD.

The not-for-profit world sees overhead as evil. It is, as I said in an article in *Fast Company* in July 2009, the dreaded bogeyman. Like the black smoke monster on the television show *Lost,* it's always lurking in the shadows, scary yet not totally understood or even

well defined. It is confusing, mysterious, and threatening. And the only way to defend yourself against this amorphous monster is to be constantly vigilant. Refuse to turn your back on it, lest it take the opportunity to make its move.

At not-for-profits, this is how we feel about any expenses that don't relate directly to our programs. Sometimes fear can be a good thing, because it keeps our bravado in check and makes sure we're disciplined. Constant fear of overhead helps us remain focused on the value and the potential of every dollar we spend.

Every person at a well-run not-for-profit organization can cite the overhead "number" (i.e., the percentage of the organization's expenses that is considered a "wasteful" administrative fee) and is diligent about limiting his or her contribution to it. Imagine if everyone in your organization—from the CEO down to the workers in the mailroom—felt personally responsible for their corporate spending. Think about how different things would be if they were all to treat the company's money as if it were their own. Would they really choose to have that extra glass of wine with lunch? Or pick the full-size rental car rather than the compact? Would they spring for the 18 percent service charge and the delivery fee for room service, or would they hoof it down to the restaurant to get that burger? Ponder how much you could save if every single one of your employees scrimped a little and helped you cut $50, $100, or even $500 in wasteful spending annually. If you put a few not-for-profit best practices into action, you could save a lot more than that.

Because of the public scrutiny of—and consequent internal obsessions with—overhead, not-for-profits rarely fall victim to a false sense of security about spending. Overhead isn't calculated annually or published only in quarterly reports. We don't receive a seal of approval or a license or accreditation every few years. Rather, we're constantly watched, by ourselves and by our stakeholders. It's an ever-present concern. Every decision that I make affects the overhead number. Every expense, every unexpected turn, every crisis changes it.

One of the difficulties with overhead is that it is calculated

solely in terms of finances. For example, clothing is vital to Dress for Success. That inventory *is* a big part of what the organization does. Without it, we have nothing to offer those women and no purpose for the organization. So shouldn't the value of that inventory be considered when figuring out what is overhead and what is programmatic? Dress for Success receives millions of dollars' worth of clothing each year—shouldn't those donations be considered a form of revenue? If they were, the organization would have a much higher total valuation, and factoring in the value of the clothing would ultimately change the cost per client and the amount of programmatic value spent on each client.

But at not-for-profits, we calculate program versus overhead expenses while often leaving out the value of the program itself—not only the clothing at Dress for Success but also the value of time and labor put in by Habitat for Humanity's volunteers, the value of time and care by workers in a senior center, and so on. Those program items are of immeasurable worth in dollars. Instead, we calculate overhead by looking merely at things like salary, rent, office supplies, and so on. Things that can be measured. Can you imagine if your most significant assets weren't valued in your key calculations?

We've all heard the phrase *lean and mean*. I think it actually refers to football players or fighting chickens or something, but these days it applies well to what one might call "not-for-profit anorexia." The Better Business Bureau's standards push not-for-profits to limit their overhead to a maximum 35 percent of total expenses. Most of us try to stay well below this figure. That's because one of the questions just about every not-for-profit executive hears is, "How much do you spend on overhead?" Donors want to be reassured that most, if not all, of their donation is going to program-related activities. They want to know that the money they are giving is being received by those in need or being put in service of a cause rather than going to pay someone's salary or to buy fancy furniture for our offices or lavish meals for staff.

We're obsessive about our overhead because others seem to be. And when I say *we,* I mean everyone at DoSomething.org, from

newbie staffers to veteran employees to executive directors to board members. We question every expense and allocation. This hyper-vigilance has saved us huge amounts of money. Our organization has a culture of thrift, a collective frugality. Our people are proud when they go on a business trip and spend a minimal amount on meals or forgo a hotel and stay with a friend instead. They boast about how they were able to obtain computer equipment for free, convincing an ally to donate it. I swelled with pride one day when a visitor to our offices marveled at how efficiently we were using our space. Okay, so he said he couldn't believe that my interns were sitting two to a desk, but I also heard him mention "efficiency" and "savings." Because that overhead question looms large at all times, people bring to bear persistent inventiveness and a creative penny-pinching attitude. It's a nice way of saying that we're cheap . . . and proud of it.

The entire entity [insert any not-for-profit name here] has one financial goal toward which we all drive: low overhead. It's a sin-gularity of purpose. We're united in a fight against that beast. What happens when people have a common enemy? They work together to take it down. Teamwork underpins the effort to keep overhead low. People focused on overhead don't adopt an us-versus-them mind-set about their respective functions; they don't fight to pre-serve their department's budget over someone else's. They're more than willing to do their part to keep the total number low, recogniz-ing that it is more important than one group's budget or one team's success.

But you can't make this work unless the culture is really per-vasive. Everyone has to be on board. And the policy has to be clear, drilled into each and every staff member repeatedly. I know of one company whose travel and entertainment policy states explicitly that employees should think of the firm's money as if it were their own. The leadership's thinking is that frugality is the norm—that employees would spend company money as carefully as they would their own. And as the company's revenues fell, employees did just that. But a few people still spent freely, as they did with their own

finances. One woman regularly dropped $400 a night on hotels, staying only in the chain she prefers, while her colleagues struggled not to spend much more than $100. The problem is clear: the company failed to save money by being vague in its policy, and the other employees felt embittered that their colleague wasn't playing for the team.

There are a number of ways your company can build a little more fiscal discipline. One way is to develop a target. Can you calculate a figure that represents your bogeyman? Can you assign a number to your perceived waste? Do you reward people and departments that limit overhead and spend carefully? Do your employees even know how much you spend on stuff like office supplies? And instead of thinking about what is necessary versus what is expendable, think in terms of what is and is not directly related to your product or service.

APPLY STRICT DISCIPLINE TO BUDGETING.

We call them number crunchers—and we don't mean it as a compliment. In my head, this is what I see when I think of one: a sweaty, grumpy, certainly deeply unhappy person wearing clothing from a bygone era and a permanent pout, grasping a calculator, stamping on all your expensive hopes and well-funded dreams with rubber-soled sensible shoes. Ugh. This curmudgeon gets all his power from making you fly coach, fill out request forms for every item over fifteen dollars, and rationing color printing.

Do you think of the size of your budget as a measure of your standing in the company? Are you more impressed by big ones and snicker at small ones? Do you flaunt it? (Stay focused. We are indeed still talking about budgets.) Often managers say they're going to "fight" for their budget, because it's their responsibility to "protect" funding for the people and programs under their supervision. And when it is cut, it is "slashed." Basically, budgeting is like a horror show or a really bloody war. It's not pretty.

Have you ever inflated a budget request, asking for more money than you really need? It's a common negotiating ploy, a game that people play with management at virtually every level of society. Federal agencies, for instance, are afraid to be frugal and feel they must spend their entire budget allocation in a given fiscal year, even if they don't need it, for fear that the number-crunchers will notice and reduce their budget the following year. Have you or your management ever allocated money for a pet project that isn't essential to the company's goals, out of personal favor or to placate a valued staff member who wants to work on it? If your answer to any of these questions is yes, then I only have one thing to say: *Waste!*

Okay, I'm not going to throw too many stones, because these things do *sometimes* happen at not-for-profits. But it's much more difficult at a not-for-profit to turn the budgeting process into a real-life version of Grand Theft Auto, thanks to some of the regulations and traditions that typically guide our practices.

When someone donates money to a not-for-profit, he may choose to designate the money for a specific program or expense. For example, you can give money to the local Girl Scouts and request that it be used to teach them financial literacy. Or you can give to your alma mater and request that the funds be spent to hire a French chef for the cafeteria. (This is true. One of the colleges at Oxford University reportedly received such a gift.) The organization must use the money for that purpose, though it also has the option to ask the donor to change her purpose or else to return the funds. This is called "restricted funding." Auditors not only track the spending of these gifts but also seek written confirmation from donors that they are satisfied with the way those designated funds were used. Should the auditor find any excess or any indication that the funds were used in a manner not in keeping with the intent of the donation, the donor has the option of requesting that the monies be returned.

Not-for-profits much prefer to receive unrestricted funds, which we can use for any purpose we deem necessary—and which we sometimes call the "keep the lights on" money. Unrestricted funds

can be used to pay for all that overhead. But they can also be used to cover things that don't have directed funding of their own. For example, a not-for-profit homeless shelter might also run a needle exchange program. It's not the most glamorous of programs, and it's a tough sell to many donors. Corporations typically don't want to be seen as supporting drug use of any kind, and a gala that raised money for clean syringes would be quite a weird party. So how would the organization fund this important program? With unrestricted funds.

As you might imagine, balancing restricted with unrestricted funds in the budgeting process can be difficult. The upside, though, is that it imposes on the process a discipline that reflects financial prudence and a knowledge of our accounts that, frankly, I sometimes wish weren't so intimate. For example, I'm sure that Ami Dar, the founder and executive director of Idealist.org, could provide a laundry list of its funders off the top of his head. He could describe in detail the specifications of their respective grants—whether the money is restricted or unrestricted, the length of the grant term, and the reporting terms required by the donor foundation. In fact, every one of us could do this—even with our eyes closed and after two glasses of wine.

Do you know where your company's money goes? Do you know where it comes from? Excruciating as it may seem, this kind of discipline is incredibly useful when budgeting, because it forces an organization to be particularly sensitive to the balance between operating income and expenses. We not-for-profits have to know what a given program costs, or we might accept too much restricted funding and have to return the excess. We have to ensure that we raise enough unrestricted funds to cover our other needs. And the time-restricted funds can really throw us for a loop if we're not careful and if we're not on top of the books. Can you imagine having outsiders dictate to you a timeline for the use of your assets?

Achieving a balanced budget year after year is no small task, given restricted funding, inconsistent funders, an uncertain economy, and other serious challenges. The discipline that results, how-

ever, produces well-conceived, highly pragmatic budgets. These financial plans have little padding. They don't have lots of items that are under- or overbudgeted. We've got to be on target. We don't have much wiggle room. The total budget is lean, with high-priority programs and initiatives funded appropriately and secondary ones delayed or even eliminated if the money isn't there. The irony is that although we aren't in business for the purpose of making money, we may be stingier than the most aggressive banker on Wall Street.

So what lessons should a for-profit take from our budget discipline? Let me throw out a few ideas that you may think are crazy, but perhaps they'll inspire some ideas of your own. First, consider creating restricted and unrestricted pools of money. You don't *have* to do it as we do, but it could be helpful in creating some necessary fiscal structure. All the profit that comes from sales of XYZ product, for instance, could be designated as funding restricted for the research and design team. Perhaps that would help incentivize them to drive sales and to focus on marketability, because their team's funding depends on that success. More important, you could use the not-for-profit accountability process for those dollars. If the sales team isn't happy with the research and design team's progress, then R&D can kiss that money good-bye in the future—and might even have to reimburse those funds. You're creating a risk-reward system.

Another possibility is to ditch your budget calendar. Not-for-profits get slapped with new restrictions throughout the year, sometimes unexpectedly. For example, consider that outlandish Oxford French chef scenario. The restricted funding led to the hiring of another full-time chef (with particular culinary preferences), which gave the kitchen staff an extra set of hands whenever that alum made the gift. Having an extra chef on the books could shift overhead percentages, which might necessitate shifting in other departments to offset the expense. What does this mean for the accounting process? Year-round messiness and creativity. And that constant shifting encourages year-round vigilance.

THINK MULTIYEAR.

Not-for-profits plan on being around for many years to come, because our work is a long way from done. More companies ought to plan far into the future too. Three-year budgets are the standard with most of the organizations I interviewed for this book. But in most for-profit organizations, annual budgets are standard, and while this practice offers obvious advantages, it often results in budgeting that diminishes or ignores the importance of long-term goals—even those stated publicly.

Given the fear of overhead and the existence of restricted funding, many not-for-profits employ multiyear budgeting in order to prioritize expenditures over the long term. We've learned the hard way that our world is rife with uncertainty: just because we received donations in excess of our target this year doesn't mean we'll do it the next. Those donations were not, unfortunately, sent in with any promises for the future. Any number of things can affect our income, from a recession to the loss of a key fund-raiser to competition (*another* not-for-profit with similar goals? Oh yes!). Laws can and do change. Even the mishandling of a major event can wreak havoc with our budgetary plans.

In the 1990s Do Something was one of the best-known not-for-profit brands in America. Thanks to its founder, Andrew Shue—yes, Billy from *Melrose Place*—the organization had many celebrity-filled events, heaps of press coverage, and an army of high-profile funders. And then the music stopped, and Do Something found itself without a chair to sit in. Literally. *Melrose Place* died, our platform was gone, funding evaporated, and the organization was even booted from its free office space in the old MTV building in New York City. When they called in 2003 to ask me to come take the helm, the organization had only $75,000 in the bank and twenty-one of twenty-two staff members had just been laid off. In my second week on the job, Andrew told me to meet with a corporate foundation that was going to save the day by granting us $600,000 over the next two years. *Hmmm. That would be good,* I thought. But what was

the catch? Turned out they wanted us to open additional offices of Do Something—in markets they selected. Funnily enough, those were the same markets where they happened to have call centers. I said, "No way." Even though we were broke, I turned down 600K. Why? Because the restrictions would have crippled us. (Opening offices in Albuquerque, Minneapolis, and Camden?!) Those directives would have been an albatross around our necks at a time when we already had too many.

I was almost fired. Andrew called me and said bluntly, "Did we make a mistake in hiring you?" I told him that I hadn't taken this position just to hold it for a few months. I intended to run the organization for a few years. Accepting such a specific and demanding restriction would have distorted the funding situation over the long term. It was a scary decision to turn down such a large amount of money at a time when we didn't have any. But I was right to do it.

Given the high level of uncertainty that not-for-profits face— flush with funds one moment thanks to a big event, then nearly broke the next because a corporate sponsor wants a different brand association—we've opted to use multiyear budgeting. At first this may seem ridiculous and impossible: How, you may ask, can I budget for one year, let alone three, if things are so unpredictable? My answer: How can I not? Multiyear budgets have helped us to avoid making panicky decisions and kept our eyes on the long-term goals, rather than being driven by short-term pressures.

Many companies, when faced with a sudden, unexpected downturn or other crisis, do a one-year budget in which numerous programs and other expenditures get axed. When you're in panic mode or at least overly concerned about a difficult, uncertain year, you tend to go Freddy Krueger on a budget, chopping away with hockey-masked abandon. Wait, or was that Jason in *Friday the 13th*? Regardless, you experience a violent abandonment of logic, principle, and sanity.

A multiyear budget allows you to prioritize expenditures. It's more difficult to make hasty cuts under great financial pressure. Your

entire prism for viewing spending shifts. You realize that though this year may have been bad, the next year may be better, and you will be able to fund a given program at that point. The multiyear model mitigates the natural psychological response to sudden downturns and costly crises. With a long-term budget in place, the prevailing psychology is more steady driving and less roller-coaster riding.

The recommendation here is to experiment with multiyear budgeting. I know it's a tough one to implement. In many organizations it will take a radical shift in thinking, not to mention a lot of work. But one intrepid group within the organization could beta-test a multiyear approach to determine its viability. Try it—you might like it.

BEHAVE AS IF YOU LIVED IN A GLASS HOUSE.

In many large corporations, financial disclosure is dictated by law and driven by necessity rather than motivated by a genuine desire for transparency. You disclose what you have to, and no more. Little effort is made to translate documentation for the layman; many financial statements are incomprehensible to the average person. Unless you know how to read them and are willing to take the time to wade through all the figures, you may not learn much at a glance. In fact, I would bet that many employees of blue-chip companies don't have a much better idea of the state of their corporate finances than the random outsider looking in.

Lack of financial transparency has always been a problem, but the recent scandals involving Enron and WorldCom led to the passage of the Sarbanes-Oxley Act, which mandated much greater financial disclosure—and paperwork. Many companies reportedly hate all the paperwork that Sarbanes-Oxley demands. They feel it's a huge waste of time and corporate energy. Well, boohoo. You're not going to get much sympathy from me.

Transparency has always been a way of life for not-for-profits. We're required, through IRS Form 990, to provide the public with a

comprehensive view of our financial information. The transparency goes far beyond anything you'll find in a 10K or 10Q SEC filing. The expenses we report have to be itemized, not one big number shoved into a huge umbrella category like SG&A costs (selling, general, and administrative). All our expenses are public—all of them! You can find out what we spend on postage and shipping, on travel to conferences, on our telephone and Internet service—the works.

For those out there who can't understand the IRS forms, websites such as GuideStar and Charity Navigator post our financial information in even simpler formats. Or anyone—that's right, anyone—can call our offices and request a copy of our finances, anytime. By law we're required to send them.

This level of transparency is required of all not-for-profits because we exist for the public good. It's the price we pay for our favorable tax status—and for some charities the reporting can get so detailed and so extensive as to feel particularly burdensome. It's one thing for an organization like mine—which has just a few dozen staffers—to report our expenses. It's another altogether for a behemoth like the American Red Cross, which has $2.5 billion in net assets—and still has to report its postage and shipping charges. (A tidy $69 million in 2008, in case you were wondering.)

Transparency is vital to our sector, because we depend on the public's trust (and investments) in order to survive. But it has helped us gain and maintain the trust of our stakeholders. Couldn't for-profit companies similarly benefit from some increased public trust?

Trust is the obvious benefit of a high degree of transparency. But there is a second benefit: transparency makes everyone at a not-for-profit think long and hard about how every dollar is allocated. There's nowhere to hide, really. You're not going to spend a truckload of money on ten assistants when your counterpart at another company has only two, because everyone will know what you're doing. A quick glance at your financials will tell people if you're spending wisely or frivolously.

If corporate people were constantly looking over your shoulder, might you make some different decisions? Some corporations spend before they think. Transparency reduces that possibility and reminds us—before we spend a dime—that there are public consequences to making a mistake.

Consider creating and distributing an accessible summary of the major financial expenditures and revenues to your entire staff. And I mean truly accessible, since the purpose is to help people understand, not to lull them into passive acceptance. I'll bet you never looked at a financial statement the way you look at your doctor. You accept that she went to medical school for four years and then did a residency, so she must know what she's doing—and so you fill the prescription and pop that pill, not having a clue what it's called or how it works on your system.

Annual financial statements distributed to stockholders and employees tend to be so long and so confusing that instead of fostering transparency, they create opacity and induce sleep. A readable, layman-friendly one-page summary of major budgetary changes, of revenue increases and decreases, of executive salaries and bonuses, and of a few other key items would suffice. Giving a clear financial snapshot communicates that the company has nothing to hide. If enough companies were to adopt such policies, then it would pressure others into doing the same. If you have no skeletons in that spending closet, why not?

How about widely distributing explanations for financial decisions? If your company decides to increase the R&D budget by a significant percentage, explain why. If it decides to give a senior executive an unusually large bonus or pay hike, announce it and make your case. If it loses money on a deal, be upfront and identify how much was lost and why it happened. It's tough to communicate negative financial news—management never wants to look bad in the eyes of their people, their stockholders, or the media—but all the difficulty is offset by gains in transparency and trust. Besides, you can also e-mail positive financial news and explanations, not just negative reports.

When management says it was a bad year and salaries are being frozen, yet executives receive stock options and other generous financial remuneration, employees naturally become suspicious. The public distrusts companies when they hike prices claiming increased costs and then see them open ten new offices or buy another company. So rather than allow financial issues to create distrust, take a cue from not-for-profits and use it to build trust through transparency.

STRIVE FOR DIVERSIFIED REVENUES.

Idealist.org receives a large chunk of its revenue from other not-for-profit organizations that pay to list job opportunities on its website. In 2009, the organization faced hardship because a lagging economy meant depressed revenue from vanished job postings. In addition to such fees for services, the organization also receives foundation support, corporate sponsorships, and some individual donations. That's what we call a "diversified pie." A pie chart that visually represented Idealist.org's revenue sources should contain lots of pretty colors.

As not-for-profit executives, we become anxious when we put all our proverbial eggs in one basket—in effect, a one-color pie chart. General Motors was too heavily invested in gas-guzzling SUVs and pickup trucks. Motorola banked too much on its cell phones maintaining market dominance. And speaking of banks, they erred by thinking the home-mortgage golden goose would never run out of eggs.

It's not product diversity I'm advocating, but income-stream diversity. An organization's best hedge against future volatility and uncertainty is revenue diversity. If you can create a good mix of income not just from a few key products and services but from a wide range of them—plus income from special events, licensing, partnerships, and investments—you would be in a much more stable financial position. Some organizations have a range of income sources, but the sources provide only token income, and management sees them

largely as gravy. I'm suggesting that you develop a range of revenue sources with the same focus and energy that you devote to developing your main cash cow.

At not-for-profits, we do this as a matter of course. The result is that we insulate ourselves from the kind of roller-coaster ride that many corporations suffer. The vast majority of not-for-profits manage a diverse portfolio of money-producing sources: events, government grants, foundation support, cause-marketing partnerships, and individual donors. Perhaps even more important, we have diversity within this diversity. We have big donors, midsize donors, and small donors; we have strategies designed to maintain and increase revenue from all these donors. We don't rely on just one foundation grant; we're always working to get more foundations to support us. We may have one big annual event, but we also try to hold a number of smaller events to supplement the dollars that come from our big extravaganza.

In this way, not-for-profits lessen our vulnerability to unexpected downturns—like the economic downturn that has pushed many for-profits to the point of bankruptcy and beyond.

Is 50 percent or more of your income dependent on a single product or service? What is preventing you from increasing income from other products and services? Have you truly dreamed of all the possibilities? Have your financial people suggested how you might diversify revenue and still maintain the viability of your star product or service? Can you find ways to generate more income from ancillary activities—licensing, partnerships, franchising, consulting, training seminars/workshops, Web-based opportunities? Are you monetizing everything in your arsenal?

ELEVEN QUESTIONS TO GET YOU STARTED:
Do More with Your Finances

Not-for-profit isn't the same as *nonprofit*. I've never run a company that was in the red. Nonprofits are places like General Motors, most airlines, and a handful of dot-coms. A not-for-profit is an organization that exists for some other purpose than making money. Still, we love to have a good year—to lower our expenses, increase our revenue, diversify our sources, and achieve fund-raising goals. Because our goal isn't to profit, however, we have a different perspective on money, a perspective that is eye-opening if you reflect on it. Does the power of zero make sense for your business? These questions should open those eyes:

1. Do you monitor your overhead? Do you calculate it based solely on cash spent?

2. Does everyone in your company aim to stay under a specific percentage overhead?

3. You probably have policies about who can fly first class and who has an office credit card, but do you have an underlying philosophy beyond "trim the fat"? Do people understand why you've got those policies?

4. What do you really think of your bookkeeper and your accountant? Have you ever had a chat with the finance folks when you didn't need something or when they didn't need something? Just a chat about the company and its history, its goals, and its future?

5. What are your company's largest expenses? What are your largest revenue sources?

6. That last question was too easy. Can you name your loss leader? What are you spending a lot of money on that doesn't deliver a direct return? I'm not saying you should eliminate it, but you should at least know what it is.

7. How many years out do you budget?

8. What would change if you reported your SG&A by line item instead of by lump sum?

9. Do you have income diversity? Or does 50 percent of your revenue come from one type of source?

10. When you look at your budget, do you see the entire company budget, only the line items that pertain to you, or nothing at all? What would be different if the entire budget were available to every employee to see? What if the public could see it?

11. Do you measure your value to the company based on the size of your budget relative to others?

10

DO MORE BY BARTERING WITH ZERO

AT NOT-FOR-PROFITS WE START with zero. All of us. Our first assumption is that we've got nothing—no people, no money, no agency support, not even computers, desks, or workspace. And yet we have to solve some business quandary or, worse yet, some global problem. How do we do it?

Not-for-profits engage in a free exchange—barter—all the time. We do it out of necessity, since it's a great way to stretch our limited dollars. But even if we didn't have to barter for goods and services, we'd probably do it anyway because barter has value way beyond its considerable tangible benefits. It provides a synergistic exchange of ideas and expertise. Even more significantly, the barter process builds and strengthens critical relationships.

A direct sale is a relatively cut-and-dried transaction. You give me goods or services, and in exchange I give you money. In barter, the process is much less linear, much more human. Anyone who has a small child understands how "bendy" we are as a species.

We're capable of stretching, moving, leaping, changing our minds, and so on. Those bendy people are pushing the buttons and signing the contracts and making the handshakes at every company in the world. We're people, not robots. We're capable of negotiation.

Bartering is about maximizing that human capability for flexibility, creativity, and trust. As a result, it entails more interaction and especially more communication than a linear transaction. In this way, it forms and strengthens relationships—between people, between companies, between brands. When you're giving me merchandise in exchange for my help designing your computer system, we have to do a lot of talking to make sure everything proceeds in a mutually beneficial manner; we often have to adjust the barter agreement based on changing circumstances; we must get to know each other so we can better understand what you need from us and what we can give to you.

If barter is so great, why don't large organizations capitalize on it? Why was everyone at this ginormous company (back in the boardroom with the cookies) talking about paying for everything— or "forcing" partners to do stuff? I threw out some ideas that they could implement for free, but their complete disregard of my suggestions implied that they felt the following:

- Bartering is unprofessional. It seems more appropriate for an exchange of goods in ancient Mesopotamia than in the modern corporate world.

- Bartering is hard to quantify. In other words, it would drive the financial people nuts.

- Bartering is untraditional. The company has never done anything through barter, so why should it start now?

Are these stuffed shirts right? If organizations have gone this long without resorting to barter, why should they engage in it today?

For starters, you've got assets sitting around gathering dust. Because of the recession, other economic woes, and shifting trends,

warehouses are full of merchandise and stores have nothing mov-
ing off the shelves. You have similarly idle people who don't have
enough to do. And you probably have desk space that's unused, and
entire cafeterias empty after 5 P.M. It's a business sin to allow these
assets to go unused. The surpluses are perfect barter material, and
companies simply have to find partners who in turn can supply a
product or service they need.

Second, barter can provide a competitive edge. In a highly com-
moditized world where companies in a given field have access to the
same technology and the same resources, it's more difficult than ever
to gain advantage. Not-for-profits know that a savvy barter strategy
provides a low-cost way to obtain necessary products and services.
Another not-for-profit focused on the same cause, operating in the
same market with the same budget, won't be able to compete with
an organization that gets additional help for little or no extra cost.
Perhaps IBM could lower its shipping costs by 50 percent by provid-
ing needed technology consulting services and software to a national
trucking company. Perhaps Bank of America could reduce its facility
expenses by 30 percent by striking a deal with Kaplan to offer the
conference rooms nationwide as locations for tutoring, so long as
Kaplan helped cover the costs of electric, cleaning, and security.

Third, even the largest organizations have become relationship-
driven, and barter is a way to create more diverse, more meaningful,
and longer-lasting alliances. The exchanges don't have to start big.
At not-for-profits we barter for office supplies and software advice.
In return, we may feature the other party on our website or suggest
an upcoming event. What starts small can become big. Not-for-
profits will tell you that some of their biggest sponsors evolved from
small trading relationships. Barter gives people in both organiza-
tions a chance to get to know each other and explore how well they
work together. If a connection is made and the relationship works
on a small level, they often take it up a notch. Barter then becomes a
means to an end. Corporations are actively pursuing new and more
diverse partnerships, but they don't always have a good strategy for
doing so—they have trouble knowing how to form partnerships

outside their traditional group of suppliers and vendors. Barter is a way to explore scores of new allies on a small scale, making minor trades that serve as get-to-know-you opportunities.

Domino's Pizza and Hasbro recently collaborated, bringing popular Parker Brothers games to the top of pizza boxes. Sprint and Dunkin' Brands recently partnered on a few product placements in advertisements. These marketing synergies are an excellent start. But why not offer Domino's coupons inside the packaging of those games purchased elsewhere? How about offering Sprint wireless services at every Dunkin' store?

Now is exactly the time to start. Every organization needs to make the most out of the least. We all need to find ways to cut costs and maximize strengths. We all need to form different and stronger business partnerships.

Barter offers all these benefits. Here are some of the best barter examples I could find and how I think for-profits could benefit from the practice of the power of zero.

FIRST, ASK FOR THE IMPOSSIBLE.

DonorsChoose.org, an organization that connects classroom needs with donors who pay for specific goods (like a craigslist just for schools), decided to establish a national presence and open its website to the public. But it recognized that its site architecture couldn't handle the expansion. Simply, the content-management system wasn't capable of handling the flood of traffic that was about to come. What would you do? Issue a request for proposals and solicit bids from the best technology firms you can find? Ask your agency to source it—or just build it—for you? Maybe ask your in-house people to reprioritize for the quarter and just get it done?

DonorsChoose.org couldn't afford to pay the sizable expense to recode the website. But Charles Best, the head of DonorsChoose, knew some executives at Yahoo! and contacted them about the possibility of Yahoo! donating some engineers. Kind of an outlandish

request, right? Can you imagine how that call went? *Hey, I need some help. How about giving me your expensive code monkeys for a few months for free?* Maybe Charles is a Jedi master able to use fancy mind tricks by phone, because Yahoo! agreed, sending six engineers, who took a six-month sabbatical to reconfigure the site.

Charles didn't ask for charity from Yahoo! As he is fond of saying, "DonorsChoose shows companies how to do well by doing good." He told them that Yahoo! would get something in return: extremely inspired employees who were very bonded, fulfilled, and grateful to Yahoo! for the opportunity. In a climate where Google was poaching great engineers, finding creative ways to keep Yahoo! technologists happy was extremely important. This sabbatical inspired more than just the six on the case; it gave incredible publicity for Yahoo! internally and externally and made it seem like a company that cared about its employees and the world around it.

One key lesson about barter is that it doesn't have to be a formalized exchange of like for like. Each party gave according to its strength and received according to its need. While DonorsChoose received a more immediate, tangible benefit, Yahoo! reaped a less tangible but longer-term reward.

In a sense, this is an advantage of barter over more traditional transactions. You can trade what you have a surplus of for something where you have a deficit. It gives you more flexibility to obtain what you want out of a partnership.

MAKE IT A FAIR EXCHANGE.

As Charles Best suggested, the best barter is when both sides benefit—that doesn't mean equally, it just means benefit. I cannot emphasize this point enough. One of my board members, Darryl Wash, once impressed this brilliant point upon me: "For us to have a win doesn't mean the other side has to lose."

The key is that everyone leaves happy—not necesarily equally

happy, just happy. If one party in the barter arrangement feels taken advantage of, that arrangement will eventually die a miserable, painful death—the kind you see in those teen scream movies. Ugly. No one should give something for nothing for an extended period of time. That's called charity. It's not business.

"Something of value" is a crucial phrase. In a barter situation, each party must receive something of roughly equal *perceived* value. Sometimes it's a relatively easy measure: you give my company $100,000 worth of consulting services, and in exchange I provide you with $100,000 worth of office supplies. Many times, however, the value of bartered goods and services is difficult to measure. In these instances, both parties need to perceive that the trade was fair; they both need to feel that they got something out of it that was roughly equivalent to what they gave.

When companies think about barter, they tend to think in narrow terms: we give you 1,000 units of product A in exchange for 1,000 units of product B. At not-for-profits, we've learned to broaden the definition of what can be bartered. Simply, it's all fair game.

DO MORE WITH YOUR PRODUCTS AND SERVICES.

Products can be used in all sorts of creative ways through barter. Let's say you're a big furniture manufacturer. Why not trade some pieces of your furniture to an overnight-express company in exchange for discounted shipping services? Literally supply your furniture to that company's corporate headquarters and all their outposts. (You might also get some signage in their windows: "Like the chairs? They're made by ChairCo.") Or if you're an auto manufacturer looking for a way to save a few dollars, why not provide a fleet of cars to an airline in exchange for the monetary equivalent in free flights for executives? Every organization with products can leverage them in all sorts of creative ways because products are the one thing it has in abundance. Economies of scale and other factors make it possible for you to trade these products at a financial advan-

tage. In essence, your products have more purchasing power in a barter system than your cash does in a straight transaction.

This is especially true for excess inventory. For many companies, inventory is seasonal or dictated by trend. Unloading that excess product might mean figuring out an aftermarket, like a sample sale or an outlet store. You still have to pay the shipping, labor, and so on, but you're adding to your retail sales because people who love the expensive ties you make may not buy this season's tie at full price if they can score last season's tie via a discounter online at half the price. So why not barter? One of your tie company's big expenses is probably paper—for wrapping, receipts, catalogues, and so on. Why not call up your paper supplier and ask him if he wants two thousand ties in exchange for free paper for a month? He just scored a high-end holiday gift for his employees, and you took an expense off your books too. Dress for Success was brilliant at taking advantage of the "last season" phenomenon. Companies from Dana Buchman to Nine West gave us last season's merchandise, so long as we picked up the stuff and gave them a tax deduction.

A *New York Times* piece in November 2008 noted that the cash-strapped turn to barter to unload their excess inventory because "a business can find new customers and use excess capacity . . . a satisfied barter partner often refers cash-paying customers and . . . the participants can conserve hard-to-come-by cash."

What are your "excess" products? First think of the thing you actually make—those ties. But you also have a database of companies that sell your ties. Chances are that a start-up tie clip company wants to buy your "list"—of your customers, your suppliers, etc. Not-for-profits sell their donor lists all the time. Several museums have realized that their patrons are consumers of the arts more generally, and so the local symphony has purchased that list—or an organization that advocates on behalf of artists has purchased that list. (If you are now worried that your name has been sold to a zillion organizations, know that some of us have privacy policies that safeguard the names of people who donate to us.)

OFFER CONSULTING SERVICES.

Not-for-profits know better than most that knowledge is power. Sometimes knowledge is all we've got! We have deep expertise in a particular cause area—like diabetes or voter turnout in a certain district. Other not-for-profits as well as corporations are interested in acquiring the knowledge we've accumulated, and so we're in a position to barter consulting for a variety of products and services or maybe cash.

Teach For America operates in twenty-seven districts in the United States. It has accumulated a lot of knowledge about recruiting and training great teachers. Other school districts covet this knowledge, so Teach For America set up a division that offers consulting services to other school districts for a fee. It's a brilliant means of monetizing their core competency.

For-profits can do the same. You possess high levels of expertise in a variety of areas—software, strategy, human resources—that other companies would love to learn. Why not help organizations in noncompetitive sectors apply your expertise? In turn, you could receive expertise in areas where you're not as strong or perhaps product or even a consulting fee.

THINK OF YOUR PEOPLE AS RESOURCES TO BARTER.

You know the old adage about if life gives you lemons, make lemonade? At not-for-profits we make lemon squares, lemon chicken, and lemon meringue pie, and then we compost the rind and use it in our garden to grow some cucumbers. We think of every one of our employees as a fat, ripe, juicy lemon.

Barter your technology guru for another company's manufacturing expert. You can trade people (who don't have a lot to do or aren't critical at a certain time of year) to another company that has people in similar situations but with different skills. Companies can also do like-unlike barter deals, trading people for products,

services, or consulting work, as Charles Best did at DonorsChoose. Does your neighbor need a bookkeeper, but only part time? And you need more office space? You smile in the parking lot but have never spoken. Maybe it's time to talk! The key is recognizing that people are valuable and versatile barter fodder.

People-barter programs can have training goals—you want your marketing head to work at Company B for a few months so he can learn from the master of branding. More often, however, people-barter is designed to help accomplish a specific task or provide skills where you're temporarily deficient. Not-for-profits often don't possess all the people-resources we need under one roof, so it makes sense to trade people with other not-for-profits. We'll call in a favor and ask for a mentorship or a volunteer long before we think about hiring a new person to fill a gap.

Creative not-for-profits can offer corporations valuable training grounds for their young people. Organizations like the Lawyers Alliance for New York match not-for-profits with eager pro bono counsel. This means that big (and small) law firms donate their services to not-for-profits. Most of the time young attorneys log the hours. Ad firms also take on pro bono work, often assigning young people to cut their teeth on our campaigns. We're okay with having these talented young people learn on our dime. We provide them with a terrific opportunity to do award-winning work, and to take chances that a paying client might not appreciate, while giving them direction and experience. In turn, they provide us with specialized services that we might not otherwise be able to afford.

In today's downsized corporate world, people-resources can be in short supply. Do you still have the budget to hire everyone you require—*when* you need them? Maybe you're upgrading information systems and you need some specialized IT people to facilitate a transition to a new system. Is your first instinct to hire someone? Outsource it to another firm? Maybe your first call ought to be to other companies on your block or to your friend from college at a totally unrelated business, but you know he could use a few days of help from your graphic design team. Or maybe your project could

be the "practice job" that a new start-up is looking for in order to make a name for itself. Start thinking like a not-for-profit. Think about leveraging those people.

EXPAND YOUR REPUTATION BY BORROWING SOMEONE ELSE'S.

Remember when your mom told you to be careful about being seen with those bad kids with the tattoos who drove a van (which had funny-smelling smoke coming out of it)? She wasn't just worried that you would come home tattooed and stoned. She was also worried that you'd be perceived as one of *those* kids. Your mom was right: your reputation is affected by the company you keep.

In Chapter 5, I talked about creating meaning for customers by borrowing the glow of a charitable cause. And really, cause marketing is a form of reputational barter that not-for-profits employ; someone gives us money or products, and we give them the halo of our entity. So Yoplait gives Susan G. Komen millions of dollars, and a pink ribbon goes on the outside of yogurt cups, helping those women in grocery stores make the decision to buy Yoplait instead of some other yogurt that doesn't appear to support breast cancer research. This is cause marketing. It is trading on the goodwill of a brand.

But reputational barter can be broader than just cause marketing. Not-for-profits have other reputational assets. An organization's brand can sing classy expensive or demonstrate in-depth science background, or it can speak legitimate Bronx. You have your name and essence to trade. Obviously, you need to be careful with whom you trade your name—we don't want to be associated with some organizations, even if they might benefit from partnering with us. We also have to be careful about how we let other organizations use our name so we don't just sell our likeness to the highest bidder. With these provisos, however, as in cause marketing, we're able to lend our reputation to help garner something we also need in exchange.

Mary Wittenberg, CEO of New York Road Runners, receives a practical service from UPS in return for reputation enhancement. On marathon day each November, New York Road Runners needs help in transporting forty thousand runners' pieces of baggage from the starting point in Staten Island to the finish lines in Central Park—it needs trucks, drivers, and systems. The cost of this service, however, is beyond the not-for-profit's budget. So UPS provides the services in exchange for the opportunity to have its name associated with the marathon. Millions of people see the UPS trucks lined up along the marathon route at the finish line, and the association is highly positive for UPS. Does UPS care about running? Maybe. More likely the marathon connotes excellence in service. Can you imagine planning a marathon in New York City? Shutting down more than twenty-six miles of public streets?! The New York Road Runners has a reputation for execution. It's a classy marathon. UPS wants to be associated with that kind of service excellence.

It's similar to that Domino's-Hasbro example I mentioned at the start of the chapter. Two disparate companies—pizza and board games? But both want to be associated with family time and fun. Connecting the brands emphasizes that brand positioning for each.

DEFINE THE PARTNERSHIP CLEARLY.

Barter may seem simple, but it's wise to enter into it strategically. You're not just swapping a pair of old shoes for a secondhand jacket. If you start trading goods and services without analyzing what you're offering and what you need to receive in exchange, you probably won't be satisfied with the arrangement. Similarly, if you don't set up some rules around the agreement and revisit them periodically, barter probably won't work for you.

Not-for-profits have been doing barter for a long time. The following six "rules" seem to govern success.

▶ **Identify your core competencies.**

Ask yourself what the company does well or possesses in abun-
dance. Think about your answer in broad-based terms. Maybe you
have a terrific customer service system. Perhaps your finance team
is highly skilled at collecting receivables. Maybe you have a fleet of
corporate jets. What products, services, and knowledge do you have
that you're especially proud of or that you have a lot of? This is what
you have to barter.

Don't limit yourself when you're considering these competen-
cies. You can leverage all sorts of assets—human and material—in
a barter arrangement. Maybe you have additional office space that
you can give to a rapidly expanding consulting group, and in return
they'll share their expertise with you. You might also have a piece of
technology that will be useful in trade. If it's highly valued and you
can spare some of it, it will make excellent barter.

Adam Sterling, for instance, realized the value in his team's
consulting talents. Having focused for years on divesting from the
Sudan, his people deeply understand the politics of money in a
conflict region. By creating a financial advising arm of the Sudan
Divestment Task Force, Sterling is able to offer meaningful advice
to companies, journalists, and others interested in their financial
expertise. He is able to trade brain power for valuable products or
income.

▶ **Identify your core incompetencies.**

What are your needs or weaknesses? Identify what you want in ex-
change for your competencies. This requires a harsh assessment, an
acknowledgment that others have products, services, or knowledge
superior to your own. In some instances, you may lack these things
because you can't afford to pay a premium price for them. In other
instances, you're not quite sure where to get them. Some companies
also delude themselves into believing that a weakness is a strength
or that they don't need a particular set of skills or type of product.

▶ **Search for matches.**

Barter requires some legwork. Unlike buyers in a traditional sales transaction, you don't have three possible vendors to contact or specific factors (price, cost, or speed) to evaluate a vendor. Instead, what you're looking for is a good trading partner. This means they need what you have and you need what they have.

We like to look at the people we already know. Try looking nearby, physically. Do you have a building neighbor? Another company in your office complex? Maybe someone you know from another context—a friend from college, a parent of a kid at school—has what you need. Maybe you already have a trusting relationship with someone in a different sphere. Or maybe you want to simply upload a question on LinkedIn and see who in your network has the structured finance knowledge you're seeking or would offer to paint your office walls in exchange for a desk to sit at and launch his painting business.

▶ **Formalize the barter arrangement.**

People assume that not-for-profits are loosey-goosey when it comes to formalizing deals. It's a myth. Remember those pro bono attorneys I mentioned? Well, when you don't pay for your legal counsel, you don't feel so bad about giving them more work. And since we don't pay by the hour, we paper up everything!

Don't enter into these arrangements as if you were piling leftovers on your plate, covering them with ketchup, and calling it a meal. If you don't spell out and agree to terms at the start, the possibility of future disagreements increases exponentially—especially because you are trading dissimilar things in untraditional ways. If you don't have an understanding from the beginning about what you will give and get and how it will be given and gotten, then you're asking for trouble. Formalizing the terms makes it much easier to keep both parties happy.

▶ **Monitor its progress.**

Barter arrangements can be fluid, meandering along with chang-
ing requirements and business situations. Check in. What starts
out great may not stay great. Set up some informal measures to as-
sess whether the arrangement is proceeding to your satisfaction. If
you're receiving a product, is the quality of that product consistently
high? If you're providing services, does your partner feel that they
continue to address their needs? Make sure someone is appointed
to manage and monitor the barter process, since this responsibility
can easily slip between the cracks.

▶ **Make adjustments.**

Suppose, based on your monitoring, something must be changed.
Do you feel taken advantage of? Does the other party feel the same?
Is there a way to change the terms of the arrangement so it's more
equitable?

 In some instances, you may determine it's time to end the
arrangement—there's too much bickering and unhappiness for it to
continue. In other situations, it may be time to capitalize on an ideal
relationship. You may want to provide more of what you're giving
and receive more in return. Or you may decide that it's worth enter-
ing into other, bigger deals together because of the good chemistry
and positive results.

ELEVEN QUESTIONS TO GET YOU STARTED:
Do More by Bartering with Zero

This concept of starting with "nothing" may be the most wild idea
in this book. Zilch can make you go, *Huh?* Maybe that's a reason to
read this chapter twice.

 Every company once started with zero, but at some point it be-

came accustomed to having sufficient money, people, and "stuff." Rekindle the creativity that existed during that early phase, the "nothing" moment at the beginning when all your company had was an idea. Not-for-profits know that we can't throw money around to make our organizations hum, and we approach every problem, new opportunity, and day of work from that point of view. Instead of "zero," you might think of this strategy as doing more with everything you've got. Start by asking yourself:

1. Do you have excess inventory? Instead of marketing it down or warehousing it, is there someone out there who might need it for some other purpose?

2. Do you have extra space you're not using?

3. Are your people idle? What skills do they have that might be leveraged?

4. Are there companies nearby—even if they make baked goods and you're an accounting firm—that you ought to talk to? Just sharing corporate pain points in casual conversation could lead to something.

5. Have you reached beyond your neighbors? Have you asked questions of your social networks, like LinkedIn? (Nobody is going to answer your quest for partnership unless you ask.)

6. Have you registered on barter exchanges like ITEX and U-Exchange.com?

7. Have you reviewed your current barter arrangements? Could you be exchanging more stuff? Are all parties satisfied?

8. Is there something that your target consumer needs—an item, an emotion, an itch scratched—that someone else is filling? Can you strike a relationship with them?

9. Is there a liability on your books that you can cancel via the delivery of your products or services? Would your accountant accept payment from you in the form of free hotel rooms at your resort or a free holiday party at your restaurant?

10. Do you think of barter as desperation? Get over that bias. Barter is smart business.

11. Use everything. What can you get in exchange for this book?

11

DO MORE WITH INNOVATION

I ONCE MET DONALD TRUMP,* and he asked me, "Oh. So you're in the not-for-profit sector. You don't find that boring?"

No, Mr. Trump, I'm not bored. We've got plenty of problems to solve in the world, a sense of urgency to do it, and a lack of funds to do it with. For some people, this combination would be a killer—frustrating or impossible or *boring,* to use Donald Trump's word. But for people like me, it's the opposite of boring. In fact, it's a cocktail that drives creativity and fresh ideas. (I then asked him what he did for a living and if he found it interesting. Seriously.)

When it comes to innovation, not-for-profits aren't the first type of organization that comes to mind. The misconception is that not-for-profits don't have to be innovative, that we aren't ambitious, and that we can simply rely on hard work and commitment and we'll do just fine.

* I was seated next to him at the opening night of Ibsen's *A Doll's House* in New York City.

Actually, innovation is a constant in not-for-profits. Sometimes it doesn't arrive through a formal process. We don't rely on special retreats or on Madison Avenue consulting firms to generate it; we don't reserve it for specific times or places. Instead, it's an integral aspect of our daily functioning. Not-for-profits have to be innovative continuously in order to survive. We need to be creative in order to keep costs down, to find fresh sources of funding, to energize our own overworked, underpaid staffers, and to figure out an original way to put on an annual event. Without an abundance of resources or manpower, innovation is a way of life.

It's not just such large name-brand successes but also the little entities that demonstrate the innovation that pervades the not-for-profit sector. Twelve-year-old Pat Pedraja had leukemia and needed a bone marrow transplant, but he was having trouble finding a match. Pat is half Cuban, and there were not a lot of Hispanic donors in the registry. Fortunately he did find a match, and when he started to feel stronger, he asked his mom, "I want to get more Hispanics on that donor list. Can we go around the country and ask people to become donors?" He had no business plan. No organization planned his trip. He had no budget. In fact, to pay for the trip, he offered to write people's names or their company logos on his head—like a bald billboard. Within two years he and his mom had been to more than fifty cities and had swabbed the mouths of more than twelve thousand potential donors. Most important, a few matches have been made from those new recruits, which means Pat and his mom are responsible for saving lives.

Innovation is often born of necessity and driven by a sense of urgency. There's a lot of urgent need out there, and because of it, not-for-profits act as a kind of organizational MacGyver. That bomb is about to explode and destroy the entire city of Des Moines unless MacGyver can save the day! Thank goodness for the duct tape, safety pin, and stick of gum that he smooshes together to successfully neutralize the plutonium hydrothingy with seconds to spare. Except that our challenges aren't fictional. Cancer is killing millions, many more people than exist in all of Iowa. More than six hundred thousand die every year from cancer—that's more than one every minute. And an esti-

mated 40 percent of all people will develop some kind of cancer in their lifetime. Those numbers are a great source of pressure to innovate.

Unfortunately, this necessity (the mother of invention, after all) often doesn't seem to exist in many corporations. Do your employees have a sense of urgency? Maybe they labor in the relative comfort of their cubicles, unpressured to perform at a high level. While they may be dedicated and skilled, they feel like they're operating in a tiny corner of their corporate universe. They don't view their work as crucial for the company's survival. As one of thousands or hundreds of thousands, they don't feel a sense of inclusion or share a singular purpose with their colleagues. They don't feel that internal drive to invent something. Nothing inspires them to work with tremendous vigor and imagination on a cherished pet project, because they have no cherished projects. Sounds bleak, right?

Part of the problem at most large companies—and indeed at some large not-for-profits—is bureaucracy. The approval process for new ideas is often daunting. Companies pay lip service to innovation and hold retreats and workshops to facilitate it, but they also tend to place obstacles in its way. The maze people must run through just to move a promising idea up to the next level rivals a Japanese game show. And political realities that everyone is aware of mean that it's the people with the best connections who get their ideas into play, not the ones with the most creative concepts or the most compelling and forward-looking notions.

Companies sometimes view *risk* as a four-letter word and usually make sure it's preceded by the word *avoid* or *hedge*. They reward people for being predictable and maintaining tradition and guarding the comfortable status quo. Of course there's a certain degree of risk in questioning an old model, in thinking about a new idea, in talking to people about that new twist, and in attempting to make it happen. There is risk at every step, like a video game with shooters behind every door: in the corporate world, enter the game of innovation at your own peril! But without that risk, there also isn't any of the potentially huge reward.

Corporations don't lack for creative people—there are tons of

smart, creative people at big companies. Nor are corporate leaders averse to innovation—quite the contrary, they're constantly lecturing about the need for it. But the culture and processes they have in place make it difficult to come up with breakthrough approaches and turn them into real products and services.

The Mozilla Foundation was originally an enterprise within Netscape/AOL. Mitchell Baker, part of the Netscape Communications Corporation team, was a founding brain behind Mozilla. She and her colleagues wanted to create a new browser that "didn't suck" as an alternative to Microsoft's giant Internet Explorer. They wanted to draw on the contributions of users and developers throughout the world. To encourage and help them contribute, Mozilla set up a process that tapped into the passion for open-source software. Online work on the browser evolved, and the first Firefox version was shipped. Then people began organically working on it and making it far better, eliminating bugs and improving functionality. The result was the seminal Firefox 1.0 that took the industry by storm. Currently, Firefox is used by 20 percent of all Web wanderers.

The key to the story is that the real inflection point for the Mozilla Foundation was when AOL let go of it. Ted Leonsis, an AOL executive, had the foresight—or perhaps evangelicals like Mitch Kapoor cajoled him—to spin it out into an independent foundation. Mitchell Baker credits the extreme dedication of contributors who weren't being paid and who spent enormous amounts of time and energy on Firefox because it was a personally meaningful experience: they were filling a real void in the marketplace. They were working on something that had the capability of changing the Internet experience for the better, and that opportunity drove them to take risks, to try new approaches, to push the envelope. The combined, synergistic efforts of all these "inventors" resulted in a product that was more innovative than any browser ever created.

The AOL environment was amenable to the creation of this smaller, more creative outside team. A company may be big, but its innovation teams need to be small and stealthy. Google famously

works in small teams that are given great autonomy, which leads to enormous risk and also enormous innovation. Same with Apple.

Ask yourself, could Wikipedia have emerged from a huge corporate entity with layers of checks and balances, white papers, and legal teams? Wikipedia was the product of a few people mesmerized by the idea of a free, online encyclopedia. They were obsessed not with making tons of money but with making a significant contribution to the way knowledge is managed and communicated.

The seed for Wikipedia was planted decades ago. As a child, Jimmy Wales was obsessed with encyclopedias. His mother and grandmother ran the House of Learning, a small private school in Florida. There he developed a love for reading, and in conjunction with his acute curiosity, he used to spend a lot of time reading encyclopedias. Those books were his first love. His first venture was developing Bomis, a website to satisfy "male focused searches," but he soon sold that company and put the money into his true goal: building an online encyclopedia. In 2000 Jimmy launched the for-profit company Nupedia. All articles were submitted by users and were held to the highest standard of accuracy. But the requirement for editorial excellence created a bottleneck that stunted the growth of the pool of articles.

At this point—on the cusp of failure—Jimmy's team realized they had the perfect tool to facilitate the creation and editing of Web pages. They had hit upon a technology to allow users to create and edit online encyclopedia pages. It became known as the Wiki approach. The idea was that a less demanding submission process would allow editors to focus their attention on a variety of articles and they would be better able to tackle the infinite buildup. Using all volunteers would allow the site to amass a larger pool of information. Originally Jimmy expected little from the project and thought it would yield a fraction of the number of articles that Nupedia had, at best. But within days the Wikipedia submissions outpaced the Nupedia ones. Today Wikipedia has more than 1.7 million articles just in English, and the site is translated into 264 languages. According to SearchEngineWatch.com, Wikipedia's traffic has increased

8,000 percent in the past five years. Jimmy now challenges people to "imagine a world in which every single person on the planet is given free access to the sum of all human knowledge. That's what we're doing."

Jimmy was originally inspired by a lofty goal, and free of bureaucratic, political, and cultural constraints, he was able to turn his assets into something more viable and more innovative. He launched the site without a huge budget, without help from the greatest minds in the software industry, and without the type of hype that creates an immediate online buzz. He didn't even have the benefit of a creative cluster. Wikipedia's birthplace was not a recognized tech hub, not Silicon Valley, not Cambridge, Massachusetts, not London, not Berlin. It was Tampa, Florida.

Innovation can happen anywhere, given the right conditions. Huge corporations may not be able to create game-changing monsters like Wikipedia and Mozilla—or even a project like Pat Pedraja's. Size hamstrings large organizations, as do their functional silos, rules, traditions, and other factors endemic to bureaucracies. When ginormous companies set out to achieve a major goal by creating an innovative product or service, they often fall short. They are forced to play it safe; they don't have enough diverse voices contributing; they have to make too many compromises for political reasons. Obviously innovation does happen in large companies—from Apple to 3M to Pfizer—but it often takes place in small teams that have been granted terrific autonomy, mirroring the not-for-profit environment.

Here are a few of the conditions that typify innovative settings in the not-for-profit world.

CREATE A SMALL, CROWDED, BOUNDARYLESS ENVIRONMENT.

Creativity happens when people are constantly rubbing elbows. Most not-for-profits possess relatively small offices where everyone

works in close proximity. Functions often aren't separated by walls or buildings, and the organization's head may be surrounded by young employees with less than one year of work experience. At Dress for Success we had six people in one 350-square-foot room. We all listened to each other's phone calls and came to know each other extraordinarily well. Within a few months, we were able to finish each other's sentences. We recognized each other's strengths and weaknesses as well as hot buttons and tendencies. People can form deep connections when they work in a common space. Everyone should have his own separate space but in a small room and without walls separating them from their colleagues. Even the people who didn't get along became sensitive to and respectful of each other's requirements and concerns.

This work intimacy removed many of the boundaries that usually exist between colleagues. No one in our group was afraid to say something for fear of offending or being mocked. We had complete freedom to suggest ideas and to veto them. We subjected good ideas to severe scrutiny, unconcerned about political correctness or hierarchical game-playing. There was no room for either. As a result, we came up with a slew of great concepts for advancing the organization.

For example, we were overrun by suit contributions and by requests from various groups that wanted to host suit drives. Managing these donations was a year-round, full-time responsibility. We had to grab hold of this beast and put a harness on it. One day I just said out loud, "We should really push all these contributions into a single week." And ten feet away our communications director, Holly Rosenthal, said, "We could make it a giant clean-out-your-closet national effort, and every women's magazine would have to cover it. Such a good simple story." Other voices chimed in.

We singled out a week in March—which is both Women's History Month and the official start of spring, hence spring cleaning—named it Clean Your Closet Week, and trademarked it. We even sold sponsorships to three companies. The campaign cost us nothing. If I had been sitting alone in an office with walls, we would never have dreamed it up together.

The open-office pit of creativity is not a secret design concept. It's been used in certain industries for years (I'm thinking of the old-school newsroom), and it's currently in vogue among municipal governments, thanks in large part to the successful, efficient model set by New York City mayor Michael Bloomberg, who has used it both in his company and in his mayoral administration.

The magic of the open-plan office is really a petri dish effect. The space dictates that reactions will happen. People may try to carve out their own spaces in different corners of a bullpen, but for a significant portion of the day they are forced to interact. Small, boundaryless offices produce a certain amount of friction, and friction produces a certain amount of creative heat. Every organization can make their spaces more open and more confined.

Instead, many companies view the bullpen as only a training ground, a waiting room for the big leagues: an office.

CROSS-POLLINATE.

At the not-for-profit organizations I interviewed for this book, people are put together like a tossed salad. If the open-plan office aims to get a cast of characters to intermingle and bounce ideas off one another, then make that cast a diverse one, with people from different backgrounds, perspectives, and skills.

The staff of Kiva, the online microlender, is a group so varied in their experiences and in their points of view—but not in their purpose—that they continually learn new things from one another. Just look at the executive team. Matt Flannery, a cofounder and the organization's CEO, hails from TiVo, where he was a computer programmer. Premal Shah, Kiva's president, came from PayPal, where he focused on the company's efforts to help the poor. The remaining résumés boast backgrounds in not-for-profit work, finance, and accounting. One staff member even worked in a bike shop.

The key isn't just to have an impressive, multifaceted lineup of talent—you have to do something with it. The diverse Kiva team

approaches obstacles from every angle, drawing on all those experiences and backgrounds. Currency risk protection was one obstacle they faced. Kiva and its partner organizations in the field work in U.S. dollars, while the vegetable farmer in Mongolia doesn't. But exchange rates fluctuate. That's the nature of the market, but it creates uncertainty. If the Mongolian currency weakens, the farmer has a problem—the cost of his loan rises. The Kiva staff concluded that for loans up to 20 percent, the local partnering company will be responsible for any losses incurred in currency exchange, while any devaluation larger than 20 percent will be picked up partially by the donor. One brain could never have understood the complexities of this situation. The finance guy knows something different from the computer developer, who sees the world differently from the guy with a background in not-for-profit development. Knowledge pooled from time at PayPal, TiVo, and a not-for-profit bike shop generated the acumen to approach this unprecedented situation.

A company can foster creativity by bouncing ideas off people with divergent skill sets who are yet aligned with its goals. Keep shuffling the people who work together, keeping conversations fresh. When you're working with the same group for the thirtieth time in five years, it's too easy to lapse into reflexive solutions to problems. New people present challenges to old ideas. Creativity emerges from wide-ranging and even conflicting knowledge. People put two unlikely ideas together to form a truly original third idea. You need a diversity of experience to think in these terms. It's great when a fifty-year-old senior marketing manager comes into contact with a twenty-five-year-old techie. I call this the Reese's Peanut Butter Cup scenario: two great independent flavors that (reluctantly?) collide to form something even more delicious.

MAKE EVERYONE DO EVERYTHING.

Not-for-profits expect people to pitch in where they're needed or useful. People there have no option—or interest—in being "above"

performing a certain kind of task. Most of us still answer our own phones and read our own e-mail. At many not-for-profits the CEO stuffs gift bags for an event alongside some high-school volunteers while the office manager weighs in on the script for a public service announcement.

People who do everything frequently possess a broader perspective; they've been exposed to issues throughout the organization and remain focused on the value of a dollar, the value of the programs, and the value of co-workers' contributions. Each of us may be a specialist in a given area, but that doesn't mean we contribute in only that area.

Do you assign grunt work to lower-level people only? And what qualifies as grunt work anyway? When was the last time the senior people at your company interacted directly with a client or spent time with the engineers in their lab or sat with the design team—not the leader of the team, but the whole team—to discuss their dreams?

INTENSIFY THE PRESSURE.

I love deadlines. The notion that something has to be done by a certain day and a certain time forces me to focus. I won't necessarily start outlining my thoughts months in advance and then carefully plod along as if I'm following a Martha Stewart recipe. In fact, I'm as much of a last-minute crammer as the next person. And it's in those pressured moments that my thinking is crystallized. It has to be.

Not-for-profit staffers often feel like they're working on the edge—that if they don't meet the funding goal or pull off an event, the whole enterprise will collapse and the world might come to an end. The urgency of the clock ticking away while imminent doom lurks turns 007, Jack Bauer, and of course, not-for-profit leaders from mere mortals into problem-solving superstars.

It really is funny that Mr. Trump asked me if I found not-for-

profit work "boring." When you're understaffed, everyone is so busy that boredom is not an option. Employing fewer people saves money, but it also keeps us focused and efficient. There's simply no room for slackers in our world.

In some large organizations, on the other hand, too many people are thrown at too few tasks. Consequently each individual lacks a sense of impending calamity if she falls short of her goals. Too much time and resources placed in the hands of multiple people are the fatal enemy of innovation. People become lazy, not only in completing tasks, but also in their thinking. They aren't motivated to focus intensely on an issue, to take a chance on something untested, to take risks that are necessary for outstanding performance. Instead, they fall back on tried-and-true tactics.

I'm not suggesting that you become a tyrant or morph into an impersonation of Faye Dunaway in *Mommie Dearest*. Nor do I think it practical or humane to push people to the point of nervous breakdown. Intensifying pressure doesn't necessarily mean threatening people or raising your voice. But setting a specific deadline—and delineating the consequences of failing to meet it—makes an enormous difference. Create metrics of what success looks like. For example, VolunteerMatch might set a goal of attracting fifty thousand additional unique visitors to the website next month, or the Mother Child Education Foundation in Turkey might have a goal of decreasing maternal mortality by 5 percent next year. These specific, measurable, reasonable goals lie within the organization's core competency. Setting them as a team rather than handing them down as mandates—and putting them in writing—will create the kind of pressure conducive to forming a diamond.

LET PEOPLE KNOW WHY THEY'RE INNOVATING.

People need a reason to innovate. It's not effective to stand in front of your team and deliver a speech about the value of being creative or to list innovation as one of your company's key values. People

need more than an external goal. They need an internal justifica-
tion, a reason to push their minds past conventional thinking and
into new frontiers.

At not-for-profits, we communicate goals to our people in no
uncertain terms and define how they relate to our organizational
purpose. When they realize that they have to come up with $1 mil-
lion in additional funding in the next six months or else risk the
discontinuation of a key program, they usually find a way to dig up
those dollars. When they know a river will stay polluted or a child
will be hungry if the money isn't raised, they're motivated to find
creative solutions.

Most corporate employees admittedly lack goals that pull at
their heartstrings. But market share, higher quality, and customer
satisfaction can also be goals that drive pride and performance.

One reason for innovation that should be avoided is the "ex-
ecutive wish." A mass e-mail full of exclamation points and "isms,"
sent out by your CEO, isn't an effective source of creative stimulus.
Posters saying "innovation lives here" are about as effective as tak-
ing a picture in front of the White House and calling it home. Just
because you say something should be a certain way doesn't mean
it's going to happen.

It's one thing to tell auto engineers that they must think outside
the box in order to come up with a car that gets better gas mileage.
It's another thing to have the price of oil over $150 per barrel and
know that the future of the company rests on their ability to develop
such a car. Quickly. The inspiration to innovate doesn't come from
a boss sending you e-mails every ten minutes or popping over your
shoulder to say, "How's it going?" a few times a day. Such pres-
sure isn't person-driven—it's a gap in the market, a blank space that
needs filling.

One of the best motivators I've seen in the not-for-profit world
is competition. That's right. Don't think that just because we want
to save the world we want to hold hands and do it together. Not-for-
profit competition is fierce. Think about cancer again. Hundreds
of organizations are fighting it. Many of them have similar names,

like the National Cancer Coalition, the American Breast Cancer Foundation, the Coalition Against Breast Cancer, and the National Breast Cancer Coalition Fund—but only that last one receives an A rating from the American Institute of Philanthropy (AIP), while two of the others receive Fs for spending too much money on overhead. According to the AIP, the foundations themselves "could use a dose of chemotherapy" to kill off the bad "cells."

Do you think the Humane Society, the ASPCA, and PETA all hang out at the dog park together? Think again. Or that the Save the Music people and the Grammy Foundation and your local music-in-schools group all take conference calls together to try to save music programs in schools? Nope. Of course, the lack of collaboration in the not-for-profit world is wasteful, and there is a lot of redundancy. But it also makes those organizations feisty. And the desire to be the best is a great spark for innovation. Throw fuel on it.

For-profit companies have obvious competitors. I once took a meeting at Pepsi headquarters, and when they offered me a drink, I asked for a Diet Coke. I thought it was hilarious, but nobody laughed. Nobody.

Do you fire up your team to crush the competition? Or do you only whisper their name, or refer to them as "they," or just nod with a serious look when their name comes up? Get loud and proud! I'm not suggesting corporate espionage, but a little friendly Red Sox/Yankees rivalry wouldn't hurt.

STAY CLOSE TO YOUR TARGET MARKET.

Peter Wilderotter, president and CEO of the Christopher and Dana Reeve Foundation, which focuses on spinal cord injury, has turned customers into sources of innovation. As he says, "Our best customers are those in the [wheel]chairs." For example, the foundation calls on its customer base for best practices that can be replicable models. People who suffer spinal injury face enormous life changes

physically and emotionally but also financially. The foundation had to figure out how to help its constituents confront the tax consequences of an injury.

Instead of sitting in a conference room in New Jersey with a white board and some bad pizza, they asked the community for suggestions. A woman from Pennsylvania who had suffered a serious injury offered to develop a model related to tax issues—and has become the go-to source of advice. Wilderotter says it's important for their group to feed off the passion of those "who have the most skin in the game."

Wikipedia and Mozilla are examples of not-for-profit innovation at the hand of constituents. The lessons from these two—and from the Christopher and Dana Reeve Foundation—is that opening up your innovation circle of trust will get you closer to your end user. If that person is part of the design team, you're more likely to satisfy her itch.

To try to get close to the consumer, for-profit companies do all kinds of expensive things, from focus groups to surveys. Maybe the best solution (and the cheapest) would be just to open up and ask them for their ideas. Literally ask them to send you thoughts via an open-source suggestion page on your site, Facebook, or a wiki. Include a free prepaid postcard, addressed to your CEO, in every shopping bag. Or consider that jetBlue's founder, David Neeleman, reportedly took a flight once a week so that he regularly mingled with passengers and experienced being one, and now his successor, CEO Dave Barger, does the same.

DON'T SIDELINE INNOVATION.

Innovation shouldn't be a special project or a team-focused task. Turning creativity into an event or an exercise suggests that it is absent from the daily routine. When companies hold retreats designed to foster innovative thinking, or when they hold brainstorming sessions in rooms with white boards and compelling sayings on

the wall, they're turning innovation into an artificial, scripted process. It's like a vacation from "real" work, and what does that say about the day-to-day? True, some good ideas may come out of these breaks, but more likely you'll generate ideas that "break" from what is possible, imperative to the overall purpose, and on brand.

Many companies celebrate Take Your Child to Work Day each April. People think it's about exposing the kids to possible careers. Jacqueline Novogratz of the Acumen Fund pointed out to me that it's actually a great source of innovative thinking. If you've ever met children, you know that they ask a million and one questions. Kids are incredibly honest—shockingly so at times—and their prodding questions force employees to look at their work with fresh eyes. A child's raw reaction to an inane procedure is a wake-up call. Taking children to work is an innovative and cheap way to spice up a monotonous work cycle. It leaves employees in any sector reinvigorated, with the kind of enthusiasm that can only result from a show-and-tell event. You can't get this stuff in a hotel retreat conference room.

MAKE JOB SHARING AND SHADOWING A PART OF THE CULTURE.

Rotating people into jobs and functions with which they're not familiar is a terrific way of building a more innovative culture. Innovation really does have a lot to do with diversity of experience. The richer your experiences, the richer your imagination—you have a lot more perspectives and firsthand observations, ingredients from which to create something new. When you've spent a few weeks working in human resources, finance, marketing, and customer service, when you've shadowed someone two or three levels above you, and when you've sat next to an individual who has spent the last two years handling tech work in India, you obtain a diversity of ideas. Their worlds, their experiences, become in some small but significant way a part of your own.

Some corporate leadership-development programs recognize the value of diverse experience. For example, Pepsi rotates its leaders into global assignments, not necessarily because it thinks a given leader will do well managing a third-world-country office, but because the experience itself will stretch this person and make her a more adaptable, far-thinking leader. These leadership programs place people on cross-functional teams and in other groups where they'll be exposed to individuals who come from different backgrounds. Such experiences broaden future leaders, equipping them with a range of approaches and knowledge to deal with the issues they'll face.

SLASH YOUR TEAM'S BUDGET.

If eleven is my favorite number, then zero is my second favorite. When not-for-profits face new challenges, we typically do it with a budget of zilch. Stretching your people, your energy, and your ideas is real work. Want to exercise your brain? Throwing money at a problem is just like getting liposuction. It's expensive, it might require anesthetizing other parts of the organization, and the results don't last.

Stretching—having a budget of zero—is an intrinsically innovative activity. It forces people to think outside the ways they're conditioned to think.

The act of slashing—simply reducing an expected number—can also inspire new thinking. Wendy Kopp of Teach For America claims to enjoy the process of recalculating budgets. According to Kopp, having to adjust an annual budget is a valuable exercise, forcing her and her team to go into the communities they serve with foresight and planning. Funding challenges organizations like Kopp's to look at their mission and their market. I wish that large companies would look at slashed media budgets as a chance to delve deep. In other words, they should consider budgeting as an opportunity for self-examination of growth possibilities.

DON'T TIE INDIVIDUAL COMPENSATION TO INNOVATION.

Groups of individuals within a large organization that aren't caught up in internecine competition can stretch their budgets and their ideas to meet objectives. Together. Too often leaders encourage their people to compete against each other rather than work together creatively. Instead, they should model stretch thinking and communicate that people need to use their collective imaginations to achieve objectives.

Not-for-profit success (as we saw in Chapter 1) dispels the myth that money is the best enticement for performance. That holds true for innovation as well: you can't buy it.

OUTLAW THE WORDS *NO* AND *BUT.*

Saying no is easier than saying yes. That's especially true in larger organizations. Much has been written about how bureaucratic cultures discourage risk-taking. Big traditional companies discourage fresh ideas that have never been tested, that might not be politically wise, or that challenge established policies and practices. For managers, saying no and sticking with the status quo is a safer option.

In much of the not-for-profit universe, we challenge nay-saying by encouraging our people to experiment, to try something different, to break routine. In fact, our job is often to lead that innovation, not to limit it. The CEO is expected to be a leading innovator, rather than the person leading a team of innovators. We don't always say yes, but we try to say yes as often as possible. The worst thing that can happen when you say yes, in most instances, is that someone fails or something doesn't work as planned. Such failures can be unpleasant, but they're rarely fatal. At not-for-profits we know that if our new pitch fails to convince a sponsor to re-up, we simply have to find another way to convince him—or we have to think of other companies that might step in as a sponsor. The upside of saying yes and trying new things is that inevitably some of them work. Some-

230

ZILCH

times it takes ten failures to have one success, but if that success is significant, it's more than worth it.

Saying yes builds confidence in people. Even if the end idea makes no sense, something in the process was probably useful and worth praising. Okay, it's the power of positive thinking, which we've all heard before, and applying that to innovation is extremely useful. Since innovation inherently involves risk, people need to be confident enough to ask questions and try something new.

ELEVEN QUESTIONS TO GET YOU STARTED:
Do More with Innovation

I'm not claiming that not-for-profits are inherently more innovative than for-profits. Rather, we are, by necessity, continuously forced to be creative. We have no other choice. But the ingredients for innovation are all around us, both in the not-for-profit world and in the for-profit. We have an abundance of smarts, and a wealth of creativity—it's up to you and your organization to take fullest advantage of all the assets that are sitting there, right in your office, being wasted on yet another game of Minesweeper or Solitaire or on yet another stack of bureaucratic paperwork.

Recently, Chip and Dan Heath came out with a book called *Switch*, in which they argue that the best time to innovate is often the hardest time to innovate. The optimal time to switch (hence the title) is when your competitors aren't doing so, because you'll gain a competitive advantage. This is that time.

Many organizations today are suffering from a lack of imagination; not-for-profits offer fresh ways to be innovative. Whenever companies fall on hard times because foreign competitors can produce products and services faster and cheaper, ingenuity can help them regain their competitive edge. Too many of us these days are

in survival mode rather than building stronger, more nimble, more innovative organizations. That's a mistake, because by the time business comes back, everyone else will also be thinking, *Oh, it's time to get moving again.* The best time to start thinking about new ideas and innovations was yesterday. The second-best is now.

1. Do you feel like one of many people in your company? Or do you feel special? If you have a new idea, will someone hear it and possibly believe in it?

2. Is risk bad? Or is it sometimes good?

3. Consider bringing in a group of sixth graders to look at your ideas. Nobody is more honest than a sixth grader. The viewpoint might be refreshing.

4. Have you ever rotated jobs in your company? Or shadowed other people for a day? New ideas are often born in foreign circumstances.

5. Who are you innovating for? Who is the customer, and what is her pain point? What does she need? Innovation for the sake of innovation is doomed to fail. Innovation to solve a problem is easier to achieve.

6. What does your competition do or have that makes you jealous? Beat it. Not their market share—I mean a recipe or a package or a price point.

7. When was the last time you were your customer? Go undercover. Be the target market. Live like him. Consume like him. Think like him.

8. Create a sense of urgency, a deadline, or a serious reason for an innovation.

9. Don't create a bigger budget for creativity. Slash the existing one. Make work conditions more crowded, louder, and more frenetic. Don't clean the white boards at night. Leave everything messy and nutty . . . like that Hewlett-Packard garage.

10. Create small teams of diverse people.

11. Learn the word *chutzpah* and love it.

CONCLUSION

DEAR CEO OF UNNAMED GINORMOUS COMPANY,

You have a fantastic product, and your brand has much untapped potential. But you have become a corporate behemoth in which your people are driven solely by numbers and angst. This is affecting your ability to innovate, be fiscally efficient, and thrive. Your pricey ad campaigns have been providing some successes, but your vendors are anxious about the economy, and they've begun to worry that you won't be able to pay your bills on time. And let's be honest, they really just see your company as a big fat paycheck that's keeping them in business. You have failed to innovate except in superficial ways. Logo tweaks and product extensions won't help you break into or dominate new markets; nor can they improve your image so that the best talent wants to join your team. Instead, your potential customers are going to other companies in your city—other companies that are not seen as "old school."

So stop it.

I suspect you read a lot of business books. Your people read *BusinessWeek* and maybe even the *Harvard Business Review*, search-

ing for new great ideas and some wonky inspiration. If I walked around your offices, probably 50 percent would have *Good to Great* on their shelves. It's not working. You're not great.

What you really need to do is to look beyond your world, to think beyond the conventional mind-set that has gotten you and your company to this place—and kept you stuck there. And so I have humbly offered the eleven lessons in this book. I hope they have encouraged you to think in new ways about your company—and maybe also about not-for-profit companies and the people who work there. I hope you've found at least a few concepts that made you stop and go, *Huh. We could do that.* Or *Oooh—we don't think like that, but maybe we should.*

In conclusion, I did think of more suggestions. Do you really want to learn how to do more with less? Do you really want to maximize the power of zero for your business? Reading this book isn't enough.

QUIT YOUR JOB AND GO WORK FOR A NOT-FOR-PROFIT.

Go on. You can do it. I should say, though, that these jobs are actually more difficult to land than you think. These organizations know how to value people on scales other than the financial. We know how to find and cultivate passionate employees, and even though we have lower salaries, skimpier benefits, and no stock options to offer them, people still want to work for us and with us. There is a lot of competition for these spots and little turnover.

Still, if you can, you should land one of these gigs. I'm not suggesting that you do it so you can score a better seat in heaven or impress your mom, although those would be great by-products. Do it because it's cheaper than going to business school—and you might just learn more. By spending two years at a small- to medium-size not-for-profit, I expect you'll witness firsthand how to manage people without using money, how to barter to get what you need, and how to ask for things more effectively. You'll also be

forced to innovate without the benefit of a fancy McKinsey team at your disposal.

Can't afford to make the switch? Can't find an organization that will take a chance on you? Try this instead.

VOLUNTEER WITH A GREAT NOT-FOR-PROFIT.

Get involved with their fund-raising efforts—it will teach you how to do sales in an environment where all you have to offer in return is intangible value. Become a member of a board of directors and learn how to maximize external people, utilize governance structures for progress, and think about financial transparency. Offer to work with the marketing department (which may be one person charged with marketing, communications, public relations, and brand management) and find yourself learning how to tell an organizational story in a way that makes you think about marketing like a human being again.

HIRE SOMEONE FROM A NOT-FOR-PROFIT.

Our people may not all have MBAs, but they're talented, they're smart, and they think differently. I hate to say this, because I'd loathe losing their talent, but you should hire some of them. In fact, more for-profits should hire from not-for-profits. Maybe General Motors ought to think about bringing Zainab Salbi on to be CEO. If she can deliver services to women in war-torn countries and inspire them to start their own businesses—on an annual budget of $26 million a year—perhaps she could handle Detroit. Or maybe you should make Pat Pedraja an offer now. I know he's only twelve years old, but if he can enlist twelve thousand people to potentially give their bone marrow away, I'll bet he could revolutionize your marketing team.

Not-for-profit leaders are used to leaping over obstacles—

without expensive ropes and pullies to get us there. We don't spend money, we get the most out of people, and we're used to limiting overhead expenses. Could we be useful to your company?

Make me an offer I can't refuse.

Maybe I'd come work for you. I bet we'd have a lot to learn from each other. And I know we'd have a lot of (cheap) fun doing it.

Yours truly,

Nancy Lublin

ACKNOWLEDGMENTS

PEOPLE I NEED TO THANK. And then thank again. And again. And maybe even one more time.

I never thought of myself as a writer until I met Jeff Chu, my editor at *Fast Company*. He has an uncanny acumen for making me sound more like me. It isn't just his editing ability (which is superhuman), it's also his ability to instill self-confidence in his writers. It is a gift, and I'm lucky to have received it.

Jerry Colonna understood that I hate poetry but value nearly every other thing he has ever told me.

Adeena Shlussel, James Elbaor, George Weiner, Barry Nalebuff, Lisa Witter, Cleary Simpson, Ken Hicks, and my dear friend Matt Ringel all read early drafts and gave terrific feedback. Adeena did a fantastic job helping with the interviews and research. James inspired the finance chapter, which has become one of my favorites. Bruce Wexler assisted with the first draft and understood that I really needed to write this book on my own.

My literary agent and friend Pilar Queen at McCormick sold the book to exactly the right people (Adrienne and Adrian at Port-

folio) and endured my text messages at all hours. And those good people at Portfolio believed in the very premise of this book and that I was the person to write it.

Thanks to Lisa Witter and the team at Fenton for promoting it and pushing me to new horizons.

Jason Diaz understood that I had to miss Halloween this year due to this book deadline . . . but saved me some good candy. And is a terrific father, husband, and Wharton-alum-business-book-obsessed partner.

My parents read a draft and resisted the temptation to send me notes on typos and misspellings. But mostly they made it possible, along with my grandparents, for me to receive a tremendous education and choose to work in the not-for-profit world.

Huge thanks to Greg Baldwin, Zainab Salbi, Kate Roberts, Steve Buffone, Pat Pedraja, Adam Sterling, Darell Hammond, Peter Wilderotter, John Lilly, Jimmy Wales, Scott Harrison, Joi Gordon, Aria Finger, Marcia Brown, Meredith Blake, Holly Rosenthal Workman, Kristin Nygreen, Shikha Gulati, Lezlie Wheeler, Rogan Kersh, Linda Rottenberg, Charles Best, Wendy Kopp, Cami Anderson, Billy Shore, Jim Berrien, Dan Rubin, Aaron Pereira, Shawn Sachs, Reid Hoffman, Julie Chaiken, Marge Magner, Veronica Colondam, Rodrigo Mendes, Melanie Stevenson, Jade Gardener, John Cassidy, and the rest of the staff (and interns!) with whom I've worked with over the years, the entire board of directors of DoSomething.org, the many people who helped me at Dress for Success, Helen Chapman, Diane von Furstenberg, and especially Ami Dar for his friendship and conversation through my not-for-profit tenure. If I'm going to be a weird, not-for-profit alien, at least I've got terrific brothers and sisters in the Land of Zilch.

INDEX